I0157709

We Love You Karen From Your Friends

Elaine Fell

Published by Elaine Fell, 2025.

WE LOVE YOU KAREN FROM YOUR FRIENDS

First Edition 20 September, 2025

Copyright © 2025 Elaine Fell

ISBN: 978-0-646-72223-8

Cover Painting: *Two Heads* by Robert Sawyer.

Photograph of Karen Walters by Daniele Cerretti.

Quote from James Baldwin from: *A Dialogue: James Baldwin & Nikki Giovanni* Developed from the transcript of a conversation, taped for the television program "Soul" and first shown in the United States on WNET.TV, Dec. 1971.

Text Copyright ©1973 by James Baldwin and Niktom Ltd.

First Edition printed in the United States of America.

Quote from John Forbes from the poem 'Satori in Viterbo' in *Collected Poems* Brandl & Schlesinger Pty/Ltd.

Quote from Thornton Wilder from *The Bridge of San Luis Rey* first published Albert & Charles Boni: New York 1927.

This book is for Christopher, Polly, Johnny & in loving memory of Eurydice.

All art is literally true.

John Forbes

Because it is the responsibility of a writer to excavate the experience of the people who produced him.

James Baldwin

Introduction

I want to tell you the story of a friendship that lasted 30 years — yes, almost to the day. It was a friendship between me & a woman called Karen Walters. Sometimes I will call her just 'K'. She died when she was 43. On the First of April 2003. Her little girl, Eurydice, or Ridi was seven when she died. When Ridi's dad, Jeremy, came to get her from school & told her that her mother had died she thought it was an April Fool's Day joke. But that is a story that I heard from Jeremy & most of this story will be written from my point of view.

It has taken me 17 years to tell you the story about Karen. I suppose it is an obituary.

I could not write an obituary at the time of her death because I was very shocked that she had died. I did not speak at her funeral. Another very close friend of hers Patrick (Patsy) felt the same way because, when I met with him, before the funeral, he said he had nothing to say & he gave me to understand that it was because it was also devastating to him that she had died & there was too much to say.

I have tried & tried to write about her. I have notebooks everywhere, all over my house, but I kept stopping. This time there is some urgency to tell you. I think the reason I could not complete the story is that I never wanted my association with her to end. I felt once I'd written it out I would feel that it has ended.

Now I am more confident that it will never end.

I am 62 years old &, to the world outside, I have not achieved very much.

I have no husband or children & no career. I have never had a husband or children or a career. I tried very hard to have a writing career but it never happened.

I have been given a great deal of encouragement from some people with the writing & I have had a few things published. I even won a short story competition once & another time I had a publisher offer

1

to publish a book but he reneged using the excuse that he had run out of money. That happened around the time Karen died & afterwards I pretty much gave up.

I began to believe that writing is just one of those idiot dreams like wanting to win the lottery & felt that my life was on hold until I won this lottery. That felt crazy so I gave up.

Now I am old & I couldn't care less. But I have a moral reason to write this book. A moral drive. I think this will probably be the last book I write. I love being old & no longer caring about very much at all.

I want to express the beauty & darkness of my association with Karen. She was one of the most wonderful people I have met. I have met many people who are wonderful but it seems it is only when they die that you can get more of a sense of how particular they were.

When they are alive they are still a work-in-progress. Some people might tell you not to expect the extraordinary from life & maybe that is wise but sometimes the extraordinary just walks right up to you.

For most of this story I will tell you my stories about Karen. I am not going to tell you much about what other people thought & experienced. By this I mean that this work will not be involved with research & interviews. It is not a history like that.

One night recently, Jeremy & I were exchanging stories about her & it really threw me off. Jeremy was Karen's last great love. His perception of her is totally different. But a relationship is a totally different thing to a friendship. I am not going to scratch around & do interviews & try & find out the 'truth' about Karen.

This is the truth as I have figured it out with bits & pieces of information from people & from the truth she told me. My association with her has taught me a little about how complicated the truth can be — the way we come to know about one another & what we tell one another.

I think I am not too bad at friendships — those I have managed to keep. I love friendships more than any other associations with people. I know we are all tied up with & reliant on one another so I am not disparaging all the people that I need in order to live. But friendships I really love. I think perhaps because they have clearer limits, clearer boundaries, than any other relationships. The minute a friend reproaches you or demands something of you or tries to dominate you — that is when the friendship begins to die.

It can also die of disinterest. I have had a few friends 'let me go' because they are no longer interested. It is not as painful as being dumped by a boyfriend but I miss them for longer than a boyfriend.

I had a friend once & the friendship lasted for about 25 years. Then she started to yawn in my ear when I rang her up. It was always me who kept up the contact so I stopped contacting & that was the end.

Sometimes friendships end because people start to make nasty comments. This has happened a few times. Deep down they have lost interest & do not know how to say it or how to get out of it. They start to make little bitchy remarks & I get hurt & the 'friendship' comes to an end.

I had another friend who would keep freaking out whenever I went through a hard time. She would start ranting at me & then disappear for a while. We had been very close when we were young. After 2 or 3 times of her doing this I stopped contacting her. The last time we met up I was in my late forties. She wanted me to come to dinner & then rang & cancelled & said she'd ring back. She never did.

She told me when we met up that she didn't know why we stopped being friends many years before. I remember why. It was a time when I was very sad. She had arranged to have dinner with me on a Friday night & I had an intuition that she had forgotten &, sure enough, when I rang to check she had bumped me for a married man she was fucking. She said she'd ring back but never did then too.

Friendships are just as mysterious as other relationships though because Karen & I might have done these things to one another dozens of times in our association with one another. But still the friendship endured.

There were times when Karen reproached me & tried to dominate me & control me & made bitchy comments to me & I made mean comments to her. I think perhaps one of the reasons our friendship endured was because we met & connected when we were very young & the awful things didn't start happening until we were older & by then it was more like we were sisters.

To the Island

Before telling you about Karen I'll tell you about my background. My family & I came from Scotland to Australia in 1962. It was mum & dad and me — & my mum's parents came with us too. My Aunt was already here because she had married an Australian marine engineer. My grandfather said, since both his children were going to be in Australia, he & my grandmother might as well come too. My grandparents really loved it here. My grandfather was 55. He had a job within a week. My grandparents bought & paid off a house in under 10 years. I repeat that last part of the story over & over to people who try to crap on about how the 'standard of living' has doubled in Australia over the last few decades. Bullshit it has.

Coming here was not so easy for my dad who was seriously home sick. I was only three. I took in his homesickness when I was older. How he would sit at the head of the table with the cloud around him & how mum would talk him through it. She asked him to please give it 10 years — ten years in part because it took them that long to save the money to go back.

Things improved for him after he had gone back for a holiday. He could see the difference in the 'lifestyle'. In other words, it was a much more luxurious life here. But lifestyle isn't everything. I first went back to Scotland when I was in my twenties. I could see what dad missed. I found I loved the Scottish people I met.

But it took me till I was much older to discover that I love all people. Every group of people, wherever I have been, have always brought me what I have looked for. But that's being sentimental. It's not okay to be sentimental in writing. It's one of the most common criticisms. But it's fair enough to be critical of saying you love all people from a country. There's a godzillion of them. It's harder to love people as individuals.

Dad hardly saw what remained of his Scottish family ever again. I say 'remained' because his little brother had died. Dad was 21 when his brother (who was 11) died in an accident. His mother did not recover from the loss of her youngest son. She had a terribly hard life. She died in her early fifties. But dad's father and remaining brothers & their families were still in Scotland & he hardly saw them.

This story isn't about me or my family but there are things about my background that I think you need to know so that you can understand the story I am going to tell you.

I think you need to know that, unlike most Australian families, I came from an extended family with great aunts and uncles & grandparents & cousins & second cousins twice removed... that we all fought & adored & stayed together, looked after & kept in touch with one another for decades.

I write this in the past tense because most of that part of my family has gone now. The family that is left is dispersed throughout the country & we don't see one another much & years can go by between when we are in touch. People in the family have had children & that has been a positive thing. I have often told the children that they are the best thing that has happened to us.

When I explained the family to a Deaf friend she cupped her hands facing each other in front of us on the café table & moved them in slowly to convey a shrinking circle. Sometimes AUSLAN is more expressive & beautiful than English.

We arrived in Melbourne & stayed with my aunt & uncle. It was very nice of them to put us up. It was a three-bedroom house & there were six adults & two young children living in it. If we had not stayed with my aunt we would have had to go to one of those dome shaped migrant hostels. I remember being terrified at the thought. You could see those places near where we lived.

I don't know where I learned that it would feel like a drastic loss of status to live in a place like that. It's as if such matters are deep in people because I was three or four when I remember feeling this fear. The fear of being crammed into those weird places with heaps of other people we didn't know. When I tell people how I felt they think I got the idea of being fearful from my mum who would point to the places & say — ominously — *we would have had to go there if it weren't for your Aunt Anne.*

After about six months in Melbourne we went to live at Dookie Agricultural College because dad got a job there as building instructor & as the maintenance manager of the College properties. The teachers & staff were given houses to live in on the College.

When mum saw the cottage we were to live in she couldn't believe it and she cried.

It was very pretty. It had roses around the door — something that was weird because dad loved to sing a song when he was back in Scotland, before we even got to the College, which had the line in it — *There's an old Australian Homestead with Roses around the door* — the song is called Suvla Bay or Suda Bay depending on what war you want to remember blokes doing their bit for King & country. Even today mum will start singing the song at the mention of that cottage — even though we have not lived in it for over 40 years.

My parents did love Australia & they did think it was paradise even though my dad was very homesick. He missed his family & the very different Scottish culture at that time but he did think there were things about Australia that were paradisiacal.

I have written about life on the College before & have no desire to write about it again.

I just need to say that for a child it was a dream. The freedom & the beauty of the area.

It was like living on a gigantic farm of thousands of acres & we were free to explore it.

It gave me a taste of freedom that I have never been able to recover from.

When dad first started work there, he would go out for drinks with his workmates on Friday nights. After a few of these events he stopped going. Mum asked him why. He said he didn't like mixing with the men & being around them. He said he couldn't understand the way the men were talking about women. The disrespect they had for them — even their wives.

This was in the early sixties.

As I told you, we came from Scotland, hardly a matriarchy. Dad was no feminist.

He once argued with the women in the family that men were more intelligent.

He believed that housework was 'women's work' & in the early years of their marriage mum & dad fought about it — until mum knuckled under & did most of it. I will say that if mum was ever sick he was caring & attentive & perfectly capable of washing up. But he would usually sit watching telly, night after night, while mum cooked the meal & then, when she said it was ready, he would come to the dining room table in his own good time & critique what she had offered up.

But still and all — he found the attitude of Australian men hard to take & told mum about it ten years before Greer wrote — 'women have very little idea how much men hate them' in *The Female Eunuch*.

School

I thought about telling you this story from 'beginning' to 'end' like when Karen and I first met until when she died. I thought of the past — the beginning of the story — as a thing behind me & it made me feel guilt at the thought of always looking behind. We are meant to 'move forward' & 'get on with our lives' but I have never really understood what those expressions mean.

Where do we move to? How do you get on with your life? Then I read, in Ursula Le Guin, that some ancient peoples thought/think of what we have experienced as a thing in front of us. Something that is true & real & something we can see. The future is unknown, behind us, — maybe sneaking up. It's the future that could be getting ready to sandbag you from the blindside.

It is hard to think of the past as something in front of me. It is more frightening than the future to tell you the truth because I sometimes think I will get lost in the past, fascinated with it & can't come out & then — the present will be gone.

I think of the past years —back up until 1959 when I was born (when there was the Cuban Revolution) as a straight line behind me & then the line curves to the left & goes back to the beginning of the 20th Century. Then the line takes another bend into the 19th Century. There the line goes to the 18th Century with the French Revolution & the American Revolution & then back, back, back, back into oblivion. It's like thinking of infinity or the future. It just goes on. The main thing about thinking of my past in front of me is the happy permission it gives me to tell you about it & to forget about getting on with my life.

There have been times when I have thought — Did that really happen? Did I really know her, did I really have that life? Bizarre because her absence is everywhere. She is still always with me though she has been gone this last 17 years.

We fought a lot in the last years of her life & there were times when I didn't want to see her anymore. I think there were times she didn't want to see me anymore. She told me once that when she went to see one of the psychiatrists she talked to them about 'the advantages and disadvantages' of seeing me again.

The school where we met was on the top of a hill in leafy Ivanhoe & the first day was scary as I walked up the hill to the entrance of the school.

I walked up the hill in my new uniform with my new shoes & socks, looking down at them. It wasn't the most expensive school in Melbourne, back then, but it was close. I met Karen the first time I went into the classroom.

I asked — *Is this 3P?* & she walked down from the back of the classroom & said — *hello,* as if she was asking a question. With her head tilted to one side. She gazed right at me full of curiosity. She sat in the desk behind me in the class with her one friend. I prattled on about how my cousin in Adelaide had a party where people were still arriving at 2 & 3 o'clock in the morning.

She nodded & listened & stared at me as if she were not really impressed with a story about how very popular my cousin was & she didn't think I was truly impressed either. But I came from a school where this kind of thing was impressive & so I was trying it on.

But I did adore my cousins in Adelaide.

The culture of the school was wildly different from the culture of the school I came from in the country. The High School I came from had kids that were as rough as guts. It was a challenge to survive it. In the first year I was bullied & learned that it helped to get through by not studying. It helped to smoke & swear & play up in the classroom.

My parents, particularly my mum, were concerned about me in the new high school because I learned a lot in primary school. The primary school on the College was tiny & it was like we had private tuition because there were only two of us in Grade 6. I didn't learn a lot at the High School & mum was horrified by the schoolwork I brought home.

The High School had hundreds of kids in Form 1 & it was a terrible shock. It's sad because I remember the excitement of going to the school. Going into Form 1. Even now when I see those signs on the road saying *Form 1 Lane* it reminds me of the excitement of High School. My mum arranged to have me taken out of there & sent to grammar school (private school) in Melbourne & to live with my grandparents.

The students at the grammar school were very different. A few of them were so neat & tidy that when I first saw them, walking in the playground, I burst out laughing.

They walked as if they had crowbars shoved up their arses. The girls all sat quietly in rows & listened silently & asked the teachers questions. They would actively engage with what they were being taught. They wore their dresses long & wore thick tights that I thought looked disgusting. Soon I was wearing them. I've never stopped wearing them. The students were studious. If they weren't they were thrown out. They started this weeding out process in Form 3 (the year I arrived). There was no way I was going to be weeded. I loved living with my gran.

The girls were weeded for playing up & not studying. There was a massive purge when a couple of them tied a girl's long pig tail to a fire hydrant & they couldn't untie it. They took the fire hydrant into the classroom to keep trying to untie it & the thing went off. The hose was going crazy squirting around the room & the French teacher was calling out in dismay *Stop it! Stop it! Take it out!* But it wasn't easy to take it out with a kid tied to it. A few got chucked out after that. I have no idea what happened to those girls. But I have no idea what happened to any of the girls. I think a lot married young & had children & changed their names & 'disappeared.' They disappeared in the sense that I have not been able to find them.

When I went from my tiny primary school to high school I behaved like those grammar school kids at first (engage with the classes & ask questions of the teachers) particularly in the maths classes & it prompted a spate of bullying that was terrifying.

A few girls who were in a gang were in my classes & I guess they told others in the gang about me & before I knew it I was terrified to go out at recess & lunch time. I quickly learned to be quiet. Then I learned to 'stir' — to try to get away with disrupting the class & annoying the teachers. Soon, when the hormones kicked in, I was only interested in boys & wearing my dresses very short.

We were interested in how people were dressed like who was wearing Levis or Lee jeans. You were uncool if you were just wearing jeans from Target.

As I said, mum saw the work I was bringing home from school & started to worry. If there was one thing my mother seriously, determinedly, wanted for her children it was for them to get an education. By the time I finished with the country high school I had a few friends & had learned how to survive. Despite any disappointments with the grammar school, I never experienced any bullying there & the teachers were very tolerant of me because, eventually, when I got to my later years, I started to challenge nearly everything they said & mostly, they put up with it.

I don't think the point of being sent to a private school is to get a good education. An education in the sense of developing a passion & a curiosity for knowledge, art & ideas. To think for yourself. From my mum's point of view the point of education was mostly to get a good job. I think the main purpose of a private school education is to teach you how to be middle class. The middle classes are full of themselves. They think they are aristocrats. They think they are richer than they are. They think they are cleverer than they are. If they are blokes they think they will rule the world — which is true. Well maybe not rule the world — manage it. The middle classes are well paid servants.

Karen didn't really have friends. She made friends with two girls who were in Form 6.

But making friends with older children was discouraged by the school. You were not meant to hang out with girls who were older because they might introduce you to things that you weren't 'up to.'

Karen did have some contact with a very serious & ambitious young girl who poked at her acne with a compass (the one for drawing circles) & worried about her weight. This girl told me that if she crossed her legs & could cross her top leg around the ankle of her bottom leg then she wasn't too fat. Karen's first boyfriend Patrick (Patsy), mentioned above, said having sex with her would be like having two giant anacondas wrapped around you. I always liked the image of the anacondas.

I didn't give a shit about weight until I was about 28 when I gave up smoking. But I never liked having thighs & a bum. Curves.

I was 14 & Karen was six months off 14 when we met.

She was thrown out of school when she was 15. Just before Form 5. We were at school for 2 years together & a lot of stuff happened in those 2 years. She wouldn't study but the teachers knew that she was very smart. When we would walk around the school yard the teachers would stop us & say — *You are such a bright clever girl Karen — why won't you study?*

It seemed to happen all the time. Many recesses & breaks & the teachers would be concerned & encouraging. I went with her to see the school psychologist at least once.

The school psychologist had strange snaggle teeth full of various colours & a mouth that always filled up with too much spit. I'm pretty sure she's a deader so this can't hurt her.

I can hear you laughing Karen as you read this.

Anyway, I don't think the psychologist was any help.

I think Karen did enjoy all the attention. It couldn't have been bad being told you were brilliant all the time. It was demoralising for me! I was so behind in schoolwork & had been streamed into vegie maths & working hard to get out of that category & no one was telling me that I was brilliant.

As a child in primary school I was given a lot of encouragement. But after primary school I've never had teachers go berserk with joy over stuff that I've handed in. Except sometimes the English teachers. For whatever reason the English teachers would react very well to my rants.

But in grammar school, rather than the teachers telling me how brilliant I was, people starting to tell me that I *didn't* have the ability to do certain things. I suppose that was a good run. Some people (many people) in the world have other people dumping shit on them from when they are very small. Perhaps all the encouragement I had as a child was a good foundation. I was about 15 before I had authorities putting me down. Now I have had the experience many times — like everyone else. I am sure my mum would be rapt to know that all the lovely money she spent on the school fees went to pay people to tell me that what I was once very good at (in primary school) was beyond me by the time I was 15. But my mum didn't know at the time only my gran knew — who I was living with — because I went home & cried.

My poor gran! She must have wondered why on earth someone would be so upset at being told not to do maths! She was my gran — she knew what was important in life by that stage. But it was a shock. I also think my mum would not be happy if she knew that one of the first conversations I had when I first arrived in school was with one of the girls who was weeded — the conversation went like this —

Her: *What's your name?*

Me: *Elaine.*

Her: *Have you been fingered? Have you been fucked?*

That was before 'fuck' became an active verb. We never said that women fucked men back then. It was always the other way around. It was very noticeable when the language started to change. But you can read that stuff in the feminist tomes.

Karen was very brilliant at languages & mathematics — & emotions. I don't know when she learned all the words for them. Maybe later in the psych wards.

I did have another friend at school. She was a very beautiful gentle character. She had long wavy blonde hair & blue eyes & I remember thinking how beautiful she looked & soft & kind — & she was. But we grew apart when I grew more attracted to more intense & critical & tough-minded types. Years later, in my early thirties, when I was reconsidering the type of person I wanted to be, that character appeared to me in a dream & we were in an underground railway station & she said —

Yes, you stood me up.

For many years Karen and I would refer to the first time we met at school until the story ran smooth. How she thought I had two spiders running up my face because of all the mascara I wore — along with being light skinned with fair hair. She also said that she thought instantly that we could trust one another. I didn't think that — I didn't think like that.

Not only did Karen *not* study but she would find a way to take the caps off her front teeth to get out of school. She had asthma & had been given drugs for it as a small child and the drugs made her second teeth grow through without much enamel. The dentist would cap her teeth & she would figure out how to get her nail under the cap & prise it off so she could leave school & go to the dentist. I don't know what she hated so much about school. She told me she was bored. Her father objected to the dental bills. The dentist kept sending them.

We did have a fight once about the teachers always telling her how brilliant she was. I told her that she was full of herself. I was surprised about what she had tucked away about me that I had said to show that *I* was full of *myself.* I was outraged —

That's really mean, I said — *you knew how disappointed I was with how I did in history* (I had bragged that I was going to do well & didn't). But Karen already knew that's how fights work — that you tuck away memories of a person's sore points & then poke at them.

I was easily out manoeuvred by her.

My family were great debaters, we would sit around the dining room table and have big arguments, but it was rare for anyone to get deft with messing with your soul or poking away at sore points. In fact, my family didn't/don't do emotions very much at all. They do their own emotions, but they don't really sympathise or connect with yours. The only thing I remember about emotions & debating was once my aunt & my cousin from Adelaide had a debate with me about something & they both took it in turn to raise objections to everything I said until eventually I burst into tears. I was about ten. Then they were satisfied & got up from the table & walked off. After that I learned that when you are having a debate you pretend you have no emotions & then you are taken to be very reasonable & rational.

Karen was always telling lies. Lies about people she met on the weekend & parties she had been to. Despite all the teachers stopping us & all the consultations with the school psychologist no one took enough notice of her at school to think about these lies. And, as I said, she didn't have close friends. Most of the lies were told to other girls not to adults. She would tell me such howlers as — she spent all weekend with bikies & had been to wild parties with them.

Sometimes I would go home with her after school & she never wanted me to leave.

She was very interesting & inventive in her ways of getting me to stay. But I hated catching the train from Eaglemont Station on my own later in the day. All the other kids had gone home. I'd be the only one standing on the train station & getting onto the train alone.

Sometimes her mum would drive me home but her mum resented it & resented me wanting her to.

It wasn't till many years later my cousin Stephen said — *did you hate catching the train because men kept staring at you*? That was why. But it was so common & frequent that I shut it & blocked it out. I felt very self-conscious on the train.

I had heaps of homework to do & I was stressed about it. Karen didn't care about homework.

I remember thinking — would she really be happy to endlessly distract me from my homework? Perhaps yes — but even more it was the company she wanted.

But getting back to her lies — I did write a story about that once & gave it to her & she laughed & laughed. It was one of the many great things about her — that she laughed at herself.

It doesn't seem so funny now at all.

One of the lies was — we were in her bedroom & she was trying on clothes & asking me what I thought & she was changing & I called on her mum for her opinion of the ensemble she'd put on & she said urgently, desperately —

No! no! Don't call her!

When I asked why don't call her she said she had an injury on her belly & she didn't want her mum to see it. She showed me her belly with band aids stuck on it. I asked her how she got the wound & she said she had a bikie boyfriend that she'd spent the weekend with & when she tried to leave him, to go home, he smashed a broken bottle & slashed her with it.

I can still picture the look on her face when she told me this story. She always had a wild look in her eye when she told me these howlers. Perhaps because she thought that I would immediately call her bluff. But I had never met anyone who told these lies before & I believed her.

But when I come to think of it I did have a friend, who I loved very much, and she told me stories that I now think were lies. She was from Yugoslavia — that's what they called that area then — & she was also very smart. The adults could not believe, at ten years old, that kid had mastered English within 6 months. My dad was amazed. She was always telling stories about what she had back in Yugoslavia. Lots & lots of material things like televisions & other things I can't remember.

It was strange to me, back then, that all those things were very important to her but I listened anyway. She also loved to ply me with food — sweets & biscuits & the like. But our favourite thing was to break off the tops of garlic plants in her grandpa's garden — the green shoots & wrap them in bread & eat it. My mum would go mad telling me not to come home reekin o garlic.

Now I realise she probably talked about having all these material things because she didn't have them. Not back in Tito's Yugoslavia. And it made her feel special & important to dream up a house full of electric gadgets.

But to get back to Karen and her lies, the problem was that, when I got to know her mum, I realised there was no way that her mum would have allowed her out over the weekends.

I know this is not a nice thing to say but her mum was the biggest nag I have ever met in my life. It was distressing to hear her going on & on & it really got me down.

I feel mean saying it because I did come to like her mum very much. But I have no idea how Karen coped with her nagging. Once, when I was at Karen's place we were getting ready to leave the house & her mum would not let her leave because she did not like the skirt she was wearing. I can't remember anything distinctive about the skirt. But a battle started with Karen refusing to change it & her mum refusing to let her leave the house until she did. Eventually, after about 15 minutes of this, I said —

O god Karen — just change the skirt! And she said —
Get fucked!
Her mum heard so that was the end & I had to leave alone.

Her lying made things really hard because when she told me the truth I took a while to believe it. For instance, she told me that she was adopted. I didn't believe her at first. I did eventually. I thought it was one of her stories.

I would ask her why she told lies & she said that the truth was boring. She also said that sad stories were cliché — because they were very common.

I thought there was a connection — she thought the truth was sad.

She used to call her mum & dad by their first names (her mum's name was Marie — pronounced Maa-ry — not Maree) — I had never heard anyone do that before, call their parents by their names.

Just recently Polly, Karen's eldest daughter, showed me Karen's adoption papers. Her name had been Robyn Smith. Her biological mum was 16 when she had her. Her mum had to forfeit all rights to her. They kept calling Karen 'illegitimate.' I think they had her adopted out after a week. But for a week she was Robyn Smith. Then her adoptive parents called her Karen Joyce Walters. It is very strange to me to think that Karen could have had this other life, this other identity. I am not sure if she knew her other name.

When I first heard this had been her name for the first few days of her life, I said it over & over in my mind to see if it had a more authentic resonance than the name that had been given to her a week later. Both names have become loaded for me. Even when people take on identities when they are trying to become public figures it is hard to think what is more real. Eric Arthur Blair or George Orwell? David Robert Jones or David Bowie? Those people did it for their work & self-creation & self-promotion. But Karen had no say in it. The adults were busy creating her. Taking her & forfeiting her & handing her around & renaming her.

I should not say 'forfeiting her' so easily — her mum was only 16. No doubt she was pressured, even bullied, into it. It would have been unusual for anyone to offer encouragement & support to a 16- year-old kid to help her keep her child. We had several women in our family, in my grandmother's generation, who forfeited their children.

I should tell you about Karen's house. It was two storey & had embossed wallpaper & everything in the sitting room (where we never sat) was colour co-ordinated with light turquoise & light green. No strong colours. The lampshades & the curtains — all elegant & all matching. A lot of the girls who went to my school lived in huge posh houses.

I don't remember being particularly impressed with Karen's house but I must have been by wealth because, for the first year that I went home to my parents, I would tell them about all the wealth I saw. Houses with 3 storeys & pools & saunas & spa baths & huge walk-in showers that were four times the size of our bathroom. And all the colour co-ordination — even the plants in the garden were colour co-ordinated. The flowers in the garden were usually white. Nothing was random, everything was planned.

Karen had plenty of stuff too — like records & make-up & clothes. I didn't take an interest in these things until I had my own money. I did have a Prue Acton eyeshadow set that cost $4 & had pink & blue eyeshadow & you put the blue on your eyelid & the pink above that — just under the brow. The eyeshadow set was in a yellow case with black writing. I loved it. You can see these things in the Melbourne Museum now.

She had Joe Cocker, Janis Joplin & Carly Simon records — I associate Cocker & Joplin with her but all I recall about Carly Simon is that Karen said about Simon's face on the front of the album (*The Best of Carly Simon*) was how odd it was that no feature, taken in isolation, was attractive but, strangely, her face was beautiful.

I thought that observation was very strange. She must have really studied that album cover.

Some of the girls at my school had strange observations about album covers.

The first time I smoked dope was with a girl from school — I was 15 — & we smoked the dope & watched the movies *Godspell* & *Go*

Ask Alice on TV. They always ran these movies back-to-back then. That girl told me that when she took an LSD trip she looked at the album cover of *Tapestry* by Carol King she could see right through the tapestry & through the jeans to her cunt underneath. That was the word she used — not vagina which is legal or medical — or vulva which is more accurate. This was surely the weirdest thing I had ever heard. Why would you hallucinate seeing someone's cunt? But she seemed to be saying that there was something secretly porno about the album cover & not in her own head. I miss her — she was another one that I ditched along the way.

Once me & Patsy & Karen went to see Joe Cocker at the Sidney Myer music bowl. We had to wait for an age for him to come out. He was apparently too drunk to come out on stage & we had to wait & wait. I thought this was outrageous but a teacher at school said —

Yes he is a little unreliable I guess. I let go of being pissed off then. The teacher let me know that Cocker was bigger than being late.

Anyhow Karen said to Patsy —

I'm bored. Let's have sex on the grass while we wait.

And Patsy said in his languid way — *Hmmm... Imagine the papers tomorrow — Copulating Couple at Cocker Concert.*

The other album Karen & I listened to was Gary Glitter & I thought he was a total sleaze because of the song *Happy Birthday* —

It was all about what he'd like to do to a kid who was coming of age. I think Karen drew my attention to the sleaziness of the song & of his attitude which, perhaps, Mr Glitter thought was funny.

She would also play Vera Lynn records that belonged to her parents & thought that Vera Lynn singing *I left my heart at the Stage Door canteen* was very funny — especially when she sang about dunking donuts there. Anyway, back in Karen's house we rarely went into the sitting room & mostly took up the bedrooms or tiny TV room or the kitchen where we would sit with her mum.

Karen was doing music classes, learning the piano & she loved an old guy called Doc White who taught her German. I don't know where her parents dug him up, I never met him, but Karen loved him. I think he would have been amazed at how quick she was to pick up languages.

At one time I used to get piano lessons but it made me cry with boredom. But I kept on with it for a few years & developed no confidence & chucked it but at the time I first used to go to Karen's house I remember her saying that she wanted to chuck the piano & I said —

No! Keep going with it! & her mum & dad were standing behind her & her father was saying to me —

Can't you encourage Karen to study Elaine? And Karen was looking at me with her usual strange look as if she knew a million things I did not.

This knowingness of hers upset my mum. She said that an attitude of knowingness in someone so young was — vulgar — but my grandmother really liked Karen.

I don't know where Karen met her first boyfriend but he was a creep. The only time I met him was when she went to tell him that she thought she was pregnant & he looked at her with scorn & contempt & said —

Is it mine? I wasn't treated to that kind of scorn & contempt in that situation till many years later — the last boyfriend I ever had in fact — when I was in my forties. The boyfriends I had seemed to get worse & worse & worse & I lost all confidence in my own judgment.

When I was very young, I did not know myself very well & did not know that I could be upset by movies & would go along to any that anyone wanted to see. Then I would find they frightened or upset me enough to make me cry. *Looking for Mr Goodbar* was a movie that upset me, but I didn't know as I was watching it.

I went home & I started bawling which upset the boyfriend because my bawling seemed to come out of the blue. He asked if it was the movie & then I realised it was.

I should tell you more about her family. She had a brother who was a complete violent nutcase. I only met him a few times because he had moved out when K & I started to be friends. He had married & had two children with a woman who was very friendly who I only met once. She was on crutches because she had a broken leg. I remember her smiling & saying hello.

She took the children & vanished & Marie & Karen never saw her or the children again.

K found out that the woman's broken leg was because she had jumped out of a window to escape her husband's violence.

Many years later K told me she was horrified when her parents left her at home alone with this brother because he would have all manner of tortures all lined up to inflict on her. When they would say —

We're going out tonight & leaving you in the care of your brother — she would be horrified & she never thought they would believe, protect & defend her. He was their biological son & he would always claim that Karen *wasn't really family.*

There was a vague & dreadful story about *the fires* which was very dark & happened when K was a very young child. I think the brother had tried to burn down something (the house?) & Karen got the blame but could not remember what took place because she was tiny.

But she had a memory of the time & was very distressed at how much trouble she got into.

The last time I saw the bro was when I was about 30 & K & I were invited to a restaurant with her father & his new wife for her father's birthday. New rules had just been brought in about not being able to smoke in restaurants & he lit up a cigarette. They came & told him to put it out & he was outraged. He spent the rest of the dinner getting drunk & going out for cigarettes & crapping on & on about what an outrage it was that he was not allowed to smoke. Everyone tried their best to humour him & get him to order something to eat but — not a chance. Perhaps that was a part of the problem — he had been humoured his whole life.

After the dinner I said to K —

He is a psycho! And she said —

Yes Elaine, that's long been established.

He turned up at her funeral & left without saying anything to anyone.

For years after Karen had died everyone dragged their heels about putting a marker on her grave. She was put in with her mum & she had not put a marker on her mum's grave.

Just recently, when K's children went to the graveyard, they saw that someone had put the brother in with K & her mum. So that's him gone.

Her father was mostly absent — off earning money & involved with business. He was very much a businessman & when he & his son shared a house in North Melbourne, after the marriage broke up, he told the son that the rent was $120 when the rent was $80. So, as you can quickly figure, his son was paying three quarters of the rent when he thought they were each paying half. K told me the story & thought it was hilarious — because so typical of her father.

He also tried to trick Marie out of any money & property she was entitled to by trying to get her to sign over stuff before she knew he was leaving & seeking a divorce. She didn't sign. It's strange how obvious a ploy that is now & you would wonder who would fall for it but back then it seemed sneaky & devious.

One time her dad came home & K & her mum & me & a guy that K had met in the psych hospital (more of that below) were in the kitchen. We were all laughing & giggling & he started frying up zucchinis & stuffing his mouth with them, leaning over the kitchen sink.

Everyone started teasing him & it all seemed very fun & amiable when he suddenly came over & put his big pig trotter knuckles onto the edge of the kitchen table &, leaning into the group with his face up close to the guy from the psych ward, said —

Let's talk about physical strength.

The guy looked serious & kept eye contact with him but the women went into a flap trying to placate him & calm him down & then the guy left & so did her dad.

Marie ticked me off for teasing the dad but for years afterwards whenever I would bring up the zucchini frying face stuffing *let's talk about physical strength* incident with K she would laugh & laugh.

God almighty, those characters she was stuck with as a child — I wonder how many times she thought — *who are these people & what am I doing here?*

Group

It was around the time of her encounter with the first boyfriend that Karen tried to kill herself by eating heaps of pills — including The Pill — from her mother's medicine cabinet & her mum saw her clattering down the stairs all drugged & called an ambulance & she was taken to the psychiatric hospital. Back in the 70's, in psychiatric hospitals, you were at great risk of shock treatment & being fed to the gills on drugs. I was terrified of psychiatry up until I saw the first psychiatrist myself at 24.

But her mum was okay because she protected Karen & when one of the hospitals suggested giving her shock treatment she rang Marie who came & got her out. Karen went to the Austin Hospital but I can't remember if she was admitted or just saw some psychiatrists there. She was very impressed with a young woman psychiatrist with dyed pink hair. She started attending 'Group' which she seemed to love very much & perhaps that's where she learned all her vocabulary for emotions.

Group was a bunch of people who would meet once a week at the hospital & talk together. She met Patrick there — & he became her boyfriend & remained friends with her till the end of her life. Patrick told me Group was called The Nut Club by its members. I am not sure of the wisdom of the 'Group' idea because I don't think any of the people, aside from Patrick, survived.

It was terrible for her to see them dying one by one.

She met them at 15 & remained loyal to them until their death. The last one to die was when we were about 19 & that young woman set herself on fire. I think her name was Monique.

When I was 18 Karen came round to see me in a group house I was living in & said that one lovely guy (I met him several times) had shot & killed himself. He used to ride a motor bike. Already she had met a bikie like she dreamed of when we were younger.

Another guy — who called me 'aloof & unapproachable' when I was 15 — I'm not sure how he died but Karen told me a story about him & how he ended up in the Group. He had eaten lots of pills & got into a warm bath & cut his wrists & vomited & his dad had come into the bathroom & there was his son in a bath full of blood & vomit. Both Karen & this guy saw the dark funny side of the dad's horror at the horror scene. Sometimes Karen saw the funny side of something because she thought it was so extreme.

Karen was angry about the death of Monique when we were 19. Monique had turned up at a party Karen & Patrick had given when they were living in MacPherson Street in North Carlton.

I went back to the McPherson Street house a few years ago & it's still a dump. They must have done something to the inside, so they can keep robbing tenants, but the outside was as falling apart as ever. Anyway, Monique turned up to the party with a plaster over her neck & a quirky bloke called Jeff asked her if she had been attacked by a vampire.

Karen took him aside & told him to leave her alone that she had cut herself. He was horrified & sorry but Monique didn't seem to mind & laughed.

But when she died Karen was really upset. Monique had loved playing the piano & loved Debussy. After they gave her shock treatment it took away her concentration (perhaps only temporarily but she didn't know that) & she couldn't play so she set herself alight & died.

I blame them said Karen about Monique's parents because they had authorised the treatment.

This was quite unusual for Karen — she usually did not have hard lines on people like that. But she was terribly upset about Monique.

I can't remember having any reaction to Karen trying to kill herself & ending up in the psych hospital. A lot of these events were kept from me at the time they happened. It doesn't surprise me that she didn't tell me a lot of what she was thinking & feeling because I would never have understood it. Several years later she told me that when she tried to die she was *psychotic* & *wanted to die a virgin*. I didn't understand anything of that at all.

The psychiatrist I saw after Karen died said to me —

Really? You did not mind that your best friend tried to kill herself?
But it wasn't that. I can't remember what I thought about it.

I think I only found out much later when the drama was over. It wasn't that I didn't understand about sadness. I think I only understood about my own sadness & no one else's. I kept going off & being with happier girls. Karen always had a look in her eye in those days — she was wired but I didn't know how to read that look, I thought it was just her.

We would always discover interesting books to read. We read *A Clockwork Orange* & had to learn all the vocabulary in the back pages of the book to be able to understand it.

You keep flipping to the back until you remember the words. When we learned the words we would use them at school at recess.

Malenky tolchocks on the litso we'd say

& when people asked us what that meant we'd say —

Little punches in the face.

We quickly tired of the language & the only expression that survived for a while was *oddy knocky* — being on your own. *Chai* for tea lasted a long time too but that *is* a type of tea. But it was funny for a while. We'd kill ourselves laughing & people would innocently ask what we'd said & it was some violent expression from *A Clockwork Orange*.

I went to see the movie when I was about 18 — I went with a boyfriend from uni & he had a frozen smile as I was raving on about how fantastic it was when we came out of the cinema. Everyone got their own back in that movie. But not the woman who was raped & I don't mean the woman that was part of a couple — I mean the one that is forgotten — who was raped on like a stage in a hall. The one expression that remains with me from that film is *luvely luvely Ludwig Van*. I still think of lovely lovely Ludwig Van whenever I listen to Beethoven. But I don't listen to Beethoven very often.

There was the 'nothing matters' day. That day we were in the bathroom of K's house in Eaglemont playing with all the cosmetics. We decided to celebrate the idea that 'nothing matters' & started drawing on the bathroom mirror with lipstick & laughing — but not far into this we heard the front door open & her mum coming in & yelling upstairs — *Kaaaren!* — & we went into a flat stick panic trying to get everything cleaned up before she came upstairs. We got away with it but we laughed about this for a long time — so quickly caught out that some things mattered.

It was on a day like this she said —

We love one another don't we?

She said it as a statement of fact & not a question.

I thought that was a strange thing to say. I hadn't thought about it. Throughout our friendship Karen would make comments to me like this & I never understood them. The only time I ever prioritised feeling was when I felt bad. But she always knew that feeling is everything. I thought it was strange to comment on us. Isn't it something that you live, not something that you stand back & comment on? She understood about emotion but could also stand back & see it.

One day we were standing in her front garden & she handed me a telegram. She must have been about 14. She said she didn't know who sent it. I looked at it & it read — We Love You Karen from Your Friends. I looked at her & she had that wild look.

Who sent you this? I asked.

She shook her head —

I don't know, she said. She acted full of wonder.

It created the idea that there was a whole world of people unknown to me & unknown to her — a whole world of people who adored her.

Later she thought it was so funny to have sent herself this telegram. It was resourceful. There is no doubt the world full of people who adored her was coming up. She did go on to create it. She made friends who remained loyal to her for the rest of her life. In the time when she was very sad & in & out of the psych hospital she met some really interesting people.

Because he lived in Ivanhoe & had a daughter at our school Karen went around to the house of Bertram Wainer & would have conversations with him. Dr Wainer told her that the world might seem small & sad but the world was a much bigger place than the world she was in. We read *It Isn't Nice* (written by Wainer) & *The Bobigny Affair* — I read my copies lying in the back of a kombi when I went away with a boyfriend who was an active outdoorsy type. I read while he messed around fishing & the like. He was very nice, but we had nothing in common. I can't remember why I got involved with him & he couldn't work it out either, but it was the longest I've been with any bloke.

Emerson Lake & Palmer: Pictures at an Exhibition

K & I used to go into the city on little trips on the train & we would buy a packet of Viscount cigarettes & get a cappuccino when we got to the city. That was when Princes Bridge Station still existed — it is now buried under Federation Square. You'd get out the train & walk up a kind of underground bitumen hill will little shops at the side & then you'd reach Swanston Street. It was not until we were a little older & had some money that we started to have fun with clothes but we did love looking in the House of Merivale & Mr John. It was in Collins Street & it was full of glorious clothes that we couldn't afford to buy.

It was colourful & luxurious & ornate & arty.

One day we went to the Trak Cinema to see Emerson, Lake and Palmer play *Pictures at an Exhibition.* When we were waiting outside to go into the cinema Karen started riding on an Electric Rocking Horse. One of those ones for children where you put the money in. She was laughing & playing on this thing & I noticed that she was attracting the attention of a creepy old guy. We were about 14 or 15. He was in his 40s or 50s.

We went into the cinema & I found the music bombastic & turgid & figured I didn't understand it. I have since heard the music played by other people & it was just the way this band was playing it. I don't think I had the words 'bombastic' & 'turgid' at that age but that was how it felt to listen. Then Karen turned to me & said —

Elaine, Elaine — we have to get out of here! Now!

She had been sitting with her feet up on the seats & the creepy guy had followed us in & was sitting in front of us & staring up her skirt.

We got up & left & went home on the train & when we got back to my place we started to tell my grandmother what happened with the creepy guy & I was so disturbed about it I started to laugh hysterically

& my grandmother slapped me across the face. But I believe my grandmother understood how disturbing it is when men start following you around & being pervy like that.

Once I took K back to my parent's place at the College. We talked & talked & smoked late into the night because my bedroom was like an addition to the house & had some privacy.

She was sleeping on a put-up bed at the foot of my bed & her neck was high up on the pillow so her head looked upside down & her eyes looked really creepy & then she started on about how she would love to kill a kitten.

What are you talking about — why would you want to do that? I asked.

I would love to just feel the life going out of it, she said.

She was testing out how psycho she could be & get away with it. Or just to see the reaction she got. She loved it when I kept reminding her of this & me pretending to believe her & be terrified in the dead of night.

The End of School

The principal of the school said that Karen was unhappy in her social life & unhappy in her family life & unhappy in her school life & so he was going to break the pattern & ask her to leave. She told her old school friend — the one with the anaconda legs & the compass — that she was very sad about this & she cried when she told her but she didn't tell me. She tried to hide from me that she had been asked to leave & how sad she was. I think she thought it was shameful but I didn't think it was. I think the real reason was that they had seen her play up for many years & they thought she would continue to muck up & then fail HSC & it would look bad for them.

As I told you, private schools are notorious for getting rid of students who might bring down their results. Sometimes they frame it that the parents are wasting their money.

I realise now that I don't know when she started to play up. Had she started in the years before I got there? I only came to the school in Form 3. Karen annoyed them with things like doing brilliantly on exams but refusing to do essays & so the teachers would say —

I am sure you are aware of what effect that will have on your overall mark Karen, in their snotty insufferable tones.

She might still have been playing the game when she left primary school — because she sat the exam to get into the school & they gave her a half scholarship. They don't hand them out easily. The only kid who was on a full scholarship was brilliant at everything. I mean everything — music, dancing, sciences, maths, English — everything she did she was brilliant at it. But K might have just found the exam for the scholarship easy. I have no idea. When the school held exams she did them & did okay — it was homework & study she refused to do. So, I don't know when the behaviour began.

I don't think the school promoted a healthy attitude to learning. They made out there was a connection between doing well at school,

33

cleverness, & your value as a person. I believed this. But really, most schoolwork, now & back then, is about figuring out what the teacher wants & giving it to them.

The only area where you were allowed to be yourself was in English.

I have heard that that is all over now — in English. Now there is a set structure that you must follow. When I got to university it was even worse. I can't really be bothered going into the horrors of university — I have written about it before — but I was watching the Paul Thomas Anderson movie *The Master* & in the film we see the character Lancaster Dodd losing his temper & getting abusive to people who question him —

What do you want? he would demand if they picked up an inconsistency in what he was saying. He would call them *pig fuck*.

My lecturers stopped short of calling me pig fuck but some of them get really irritated if you ask them questions.

I am pleased to be old & to be getting to the end of my run with my involvement with work & education. Friends who work as teachers tell me stories of how their world is being taken over by bureaucrats.

But I work at a university supporting students with disabilities & I go to all kinds of classes & take notes for the students. It is the best job — I love it very much. I mean the actual work. Of course, the wages & conditions are rubbish. Which brings me to what I have figured out & it took me a long time to figure it out — you feel much better about things if you find things to love.

Quentin Crisp said this in one of his books. That you are defined by what you love. What you love is who you are. Karen loved many things & introduced me to many things. She was interested in a lot of subjects. A lot of my account so far has been the sadness of her life & this does not explain what it was like to be with her at all.

When she left school she really started to read.

She went to another high school for a while — can't remember the name of it — & then she took up an apprenticeship as a florist. She was good at that.

But I always thought it was funny that she developed a loathing for gerberas. Why on earth did she hate them? — she said they were boring. Another thing that I caught off her — before I would have no opinion of gerberas.

Funeral

On the morning of her funeral I went to that beautiful florist in Brunswick Street, *Vasette*.

My friend Katie had given me money to buy flowers. In these situations I always feel like blurting out the truth. I felt like saying to the woman behind the counter —

I am on my way to the funeral of my friend — the friend I had for 30 years —

But the only way I know how to get people to understand is to say 'my best friend' but it's not really accurate.

I have other very good friends. It could be like losing a sister, as I said, but I don't know because I've never had a sister.

A psychologist I went to see recently asked —

What is it that you have lost Elaine? What have you lost?

And he tried to stifle a yawn when I tried to explain. My friend Allie said that was a stupid question — like asking someone to describe the colour blue.

Boyfriends have not been able to understand why I loved her so much. One friend said it was not normal to be so close to someone if they are not a family member or a lover. But the writer Dana Johnson gets it. In her book *Elsewhere, California* she talks about Avery's love for her friend Brenna. I love Dana Johnson books.

On the day of the funeral when I got to the Church Hall I went in at the back & Jeremy was there. We could go into the church to see her laid out in her coffin before the funeral. I went in & I looked at her & looked away & then looked at her again. I went back out and the minister was there & Jeremy was waiting.

I started crying & blubbering.

O Yane, said Jeremy. I got the nickname Yane from Karen's first son Christopher when he was a little kid he couldn't say Elaine.

O Elaine, said the Minister — *you have known her for such a long time.*

She looks so dead, I said.

Well, she has been dead for a while, said the minister nodding her head in agreement.

I really loved her for that — for telling the truth of how things are. Karen had been dead for about 2 weeks. They had to do tests to figure out what exactly had killed her. There were a number of drugs in her system & the heroin she took that morning took her over the line. Jeremy said the last look Karen gave him when she left the house that morning was a look as if to say —

What's life worth?

What's life worth. What's life worth. How could she have come to that?

Jeremy also told me on the day she died a willy wagtail got caught in the stairwell of the block of flats where they were living. He managed to get it out. Karen loved those little birds & he found it weird that the bird was trapped. Then, later in the day, a willy wagtail was trapped again. He wasn't sure if it was the same bird but he said that he has never seen a bird trapped there before or since.

As I told you, Patsy & I didn't speak at her funeral. I went & met him before the day & told him that I was really afraid. He asked me why & I explained that I thought I might lose it — fall apart & start sobbing uncontrollably. He said —

If you lose it, you lose it.

He told me that when his granny died (who he really loved) he kept it together & then when another relative died, I'm not sure, maybe his dad, he really sobbed.

It was Karen's ex — Tim — who rang to tell me that Karen had died. He rang, we chatted for a bit & then he just said —

Karen's dead.

I was so shocked I just kept saying —

Fuck, fuck, fuck & crying & saying *I am finding this hard to handle.*

He suggested I ring Karina because he had a lot of other people to ring. I rang Karina & got her answering machine.

I don't know why I rang her. I think I went into auto pilot & when Tim said to ring her I just did.

In the days that followed I started to write to Karen. I was trying to continue a conversation that was over. It was a long time before I felt that she was gone.

A few days after she died I had a very strong feeling that she was really angry & disappointed because her death was a mistake. I know this makes no sense. Perhaps it was a protective force inside me that dreamed this up. But I do think it was a terrible accident. I don't think she meant to die.

In the months following her death my dream of being a writer was broken too. I was able to sustain the dream for ages but it was when a publisher offered to publish a novel of mine & then reneged 18 months later, & tried to get me to give him money, that I gave up. My mum was always trying to tell me to enjoy the day to day. I found it hard because I was waiting for success. Now I wonder if the day to day I enjoy is too small. I enjoy the different smells of dishwashing liquid.

Today they were hassling me in the employment office about finding more work.

I left the office in a bad mood & saw a bee on the footpath. Just the sight of the bee made me forget the madness of involvement with other people.

It is good to have old people around for this reason. They have seen & done & felt it & they pretty much couldn't give a damn. It's lovely to be around people like that. Old people & little kids.

Karen was pretty much like that for most of her life. She would watch me frantically trying to achieve something & then falling apart.

She thought it was useless to fight them. They would always win. She had an attitude I thought was strange. She thought they would see us fight them & it was just a source of irritation — because their triumph was certain.

Before I Met Her

I read in one of Patti Smith's books, I think it was *M Train,* that when her husband died she felt that she had to go back & recreate herself. Go back to the time before she met him.

I felt like that when Karen had gone.

I remembered back to the glorious summer before I came to Melbourne & before I met her.

It was hot & I spent time with friends at the Shepparton swimming pool. It's a massive pool. People kept saying — *It's the biggest pool in the Southern Hemisphere.* I suppose that means they have bigger pools up North. Or a pool just as big up North.

I borrowed a friend's leather sandals & was looking down at these beautiful sandals as I walked along — they were like Roman sandals. It was an exciting time because we had a new Labor government & my friend's mum was yelling abuse at McMahon on the telly.

She was glad to see the back of him. I was excited because I was going to live with my grandparents & I loved my grandmother who was always kind to me.

It was my whole attitude to life I felt that I had to recover when Karen died.

I couldn't figure out any more what was her & what was me. We spoke about how we always felt estranged from much that was going on & it was part of why we thought many things were very funny.

My dad was convinced that my attitude & way of being was environmental — he thought if the family had stayed in Scotland I would be married with 4 children. He was disappointed that I never got married & he could walk me down the aisle.

But when I talked about this with Karen — she was convinced that we were 'there' from the beginning — that no matter where we were brought up we would have been the same. We would have had the same outlook.

When Karen died my mum said — *O Elaine she has been such a dark force in your life for so long*. It is very strange to me that a person who I was so close to for all those years could be seen as a 'dark force.'

For months after her death I felt that I was being watched by a creature like a perversely interested lizard. It was sinister —it was to the left of my vision. It just sat & watched & waited, with cold interested eyes, as if it was waiting to see if I would survive. It was there for ages & I don't know when it went away but it did.

The reactions of other people in these situations are often hilarious because they are often so terrible — hilarious if they didn't add to your sorrow. One woman, who prided herself on being an excellent counsellor, would ask me how I was going & when I told her that I could not stop crying would say —

Still?! — in an aggressive, confronting way.

Like my time was up. Time to stop & get on with & move forward.

Karen made me angry in a science class at school. We had to be serious & we were cutting up these disgusting dead rats & looking at the rat's kidneys & stuff.

The smell of those pickled rats was the worst thing — that & their wet yellow fur. Yellow from the stuff they were pickled in. And Karen just kept laughing & refusing to take anything seriously. Then she made out as if she was going to flick some of the dead rat stuff on me &, with the combination of the not-taking-it-serious & the horror of being flicked with this stuff, I didn't see red — my vision went blurry with rage. I don't know if she knew because I only remember her laughing. I wrote about this for our wonderful, eccentric English teacher & described exactly how it felt to get so mad & the English teacher loved it.

I guess Karen helped me to do English even if she couldn't help in science.

But Karen was very interested in science & thought in that way. When we were studying chemistry in Form 4 we learned something about double and triple covalent bonds. We looked up what a morphine molecule would look like. The formula was $C17\,H19\,N\,O3$.

One Saturday night we spent hours & hours doodling on paper trying to figure out how those molecules would be joined together. I don't know why we picked morphine. I think we knew that we were unlikely to get it right but it engrossed us for a long time.

Alone

I used to love it when my grandparents went out on a Saturday night & I could stay at home & listen to the radio or listen to their daggy records. I loved their Andy Williams record *Raindrops Keep Fallin' On My Head* & I loved the medley part of that album. On the cover he is walking down a green hill in a blue outfit.

I'd also listen to the radio & go back & forward from 3XY to 3AK looking for Led Zeppelin songs. I first heard Led Zeppelin when I was about 11 & didn't understand them but by the time I was 15 I loved them. 3AK used to be great for teenagers until they went weird & decided to go all 'easy listening' which was not easy listening.

I had already developed a taste for being on my own which bothered my grandmother who was a social person who loved a party. She liked Karen. She was not a judgemental person but, on the contrary, would sit & tell me stories of the scandals in the family. Children born who were expected to be given away was one of the main themes.

After Karen died I wondered why didn't I tell her —

C'mon, c'mon — don't you remember what you were like? Laughing, *always full of ideas, always interested.*

I said to her once —

Find something to do — pick oranges for the revolution.

But it wouldn't be my revolution, she would say.

She once said —

You don't think you can save me do you? In a voice full of scorn & contempt.

I would always stop writing this story because I wanted to make her come back to life in the writing. I was defeated by the strain & the effort. I know it's insane & impossible.

I don't know if I can convey a sense of her. Now my ambition is just to keep going & going until there's nothing more to tell.

Karen used to write her e's like the lower-case Greek epsilon. I used to write my e's like a cursive e but with more loops. But I liked the simplicity of her writing & I copied her e & now it's in my signature.

I got advice from a psychiatrist after she died.

The best thing the psychiatrist did was to recommend books that were about the nature of anxiety. Reading these books made me aware that some of the thoughts & behaviours of someone who suffers from anxiety are common to all people who suffer from anxiety.

I thought it was only me who did not like going to quiet places because my innards might make embarrassing noises.

I thought it was me who started to have magical thinking about objects — like for example — I had to take a particular piece of jewellery with me so that everything would be okay.

I believe a major reason why I don't suffer the same depression & anxiety is because I got my own place to live. It may sound banal but I have been stressed about being homeless from when I was very young. Perhaps because I've never been able to hold down a job. The strange thing is that I have been able to hold down a job since I got a home.

Ivanhoe Flat

After she left school she moved into a flat in Ivanhoe above a shop. She was very keen to get away from the family home. I'm not sure when she moved in but I know when she moved out — she was 18 because I had my first full time job at the Board of Jerks (the Board of Works or now the Water Board) & one day I didn't get to work till about 2 o'clock in the afternoon because I was helping her flee from that flat. I think she was there when she was 16 because I remember that's when her reading really took off.

I think we were around 16 when we began to read everything we could by Bertrand Russell. Karen found him & loved him & called him 'Bertie' & she introduced him to me. I think we loved his clear & straightforward writing & his 'sensible' solutions to complex problems. He had kindness & humanity about him. We were obsessed with him for a long time — a long time by teenage standards. We didn't know anything about his mathematics but loved it that his advice was to write a book that no one understands (*Principia Mathematica*) & this will make you famous & then you can write whatever you like. Karen loved that he gave away a fortune & promptly made another. We went off him big time later — especially when we became interested in European philosophy & his *A History of Western Philosophy* has a section on Nietzsche which is ridiculous. But recently I have been looking at interviews with Russell on YouTube & it reminds me of what a beautiful & gentle man he was. The idea I got from him was that the world would rapidly become a paradise if people only wanted to become rich. The trouble is they want to keep people poor.

The other Englishman I was obsessed with much later was Quentin Crisp — I think Karen liked & appreciated him but not as much as me. I'm not sure if he was fully appreciated for his brilliance & his advice on life. My brother & my cousin rang him up in New York once & he chatted away happily with them. Then my brother sent him one of my stories. The things that come to mind when I think of Mr Crisp are —

- That he visited someone in an institution (can't remember if it was hospital or prison) every week for many years.
- A sense of humour literally saved his life because he said to a group of guys who were beating him up — *I seem to have done something to upset you gentlemen* — & it stopped them beating him up.
- That the purpose of life is to be involved with other people — but maybe just one person every day. So you could have 365 friends or acquaintances.
- Not to be precious about your writing — let the editors do their job.
- When you write film reviews you should try to find something positive to say because films cost such a lot of money.
- That many people go to jail & then get out of jail & resume their lives so what really happened with Oscar Wilde? He thought Oscar Wilde was suffering from a destructive self-hatred.
- That he had trouble disguising himself as a human being.
- When you've had an awful day (or evening) go home & have a good cry.
- That he was never famous — he was notorious.

When Karen moved into her flat she got some beautiful old furniture from a very interesting person called Donald who went to the boys' school. We went around to visit him in his house in Ivanhoe & it was the first time I had ever seen such a carefully decorated stylish room.

It was like something from the 1920's. Up until that point I had only been in houses where people furnished them because they needed a couch or a chair or a table or a lamp.

The type of furniture could be expensive & fashionable or new or just grabbed & bought randomly. But this room was like a work of art. We all had a great evening together.

He loaned Karen some beautiful old leather chairs & they were abandoned in the midnight flit & he was really annoyed for ages after.

This flat was where Karen first began to 'express' herself with her housekeeping. She first lived there with a friendly girl who had such a big gap between her teeth she could hold a cigarette in it. I never thought she looked bad — but she got braces to fix the gap.

Then this girl moved out & Patsy, her boyfriend, moved in.

There was a time when Patsy had an awful factory day job. But Patsy was always a musician. By the time he moved in she was established in her own peculiar way of housekeeping. She always had pet cats & would hardly ever clean up after them. She thought the cat was toilet trained & then discovered that it had been shitting behind an armchair for months. Once, me & Donald went to the flat when Karen wasn't home & wandered around looking in empty teacups & finding mould in various multi colours, rotting food, filthy clothes & all manner of such finds. Donald & I could not stop laughing. He left her a note saying —

One is never bored at Karen's — one is always finding new horrors. Once she asked me if I would go & try to clean it up & she would pay me & I tried — I started in the kitchen.

She had Trix dishwashing detergent which smelt of mint. When I see or smell that stuff I remember that day trying to clean her flat. Oof — remembrance of things past.

I guess there would have been cigarette butts everywhere too. I don't remember that. Smoking was a given. But when I started to try to clean up — & I love cleaning up — especially when it's a huge mess — like after a party or a wake & there are food scraps & drink bottles & cigarette butts everywhere. I love cleaning that up. I think it's the transformation I love. It's much more fun than cleaning ordinary homes with dust & bathroom scum & carpets that need vacuumed. That stuff always needs doing but you can't see a dramatic change. I also bitterly resent being expected to clean up when you live with people. My family are like that. I grew up with men who expected women to clean & I hated it. Maybe that's one of the reasons I've lived alone for decades. But Karen's flat was the first time I was confronted with such a task & the first time I was defeated.

I was a novice. There was no clean surface. I started in the kitchen & there was no clean bench. Every bench was filthy, every piece of cutlery or crockery was used. The floor was filthy. The fridge too. I think I might be able to do it now. I would have more determination. But at 17 or 18 I was stumped at where to put the clean stuff & where to put the dirty stuff when I cleaned the clean stuff.

But I loved visiting her & I was never affected by the grot. I just thought of it as part of her & she was very determined to live that way.

At first it was obvious that she was rebelling against the crazy restrictions that she had escaped but she did say to me once, early on, that her — *adolescent rebellion against cleanliness & tidiness was getting a bit old.*

A few times I made the mistake of enjoying telling people about her crazy house but they thought it said something negative or tragic about her character. I am telling you about it now & I am sure that you will read into it all that you want.

When I next saw her I explained that I couldn't clean it up because it was too much for me & she just shrugged & said — *thanks for trying.*

When she had children though this was much more of an issue & I am certain it upset her children. The only time I ever saw her keep it together was when she was in a group house with women. Maybe all the women doing something enabled her to keep it together. Maybe she knew she would not get away with that with a group of women.

Once I went to see her in the flat when Patsy had gone back home to Ireland for a holiday.

I hung around & spoke with her. She hadn't got out of bed. After a long conversation I said good-bye & then started to leave & as I was walking down the stairs she called out —

Why Elaine? Why?

I came back up the stairs & looked at her — she was asking why I was leaving.

I stood & spoke with her for a bit longer & then asked if she was okay for me to leave now. She seemed a lot better. When I told her this story many years later it was another one where she laughed & laughed. But she also said that when Patrick went back home to Ireland she became psychotic with sorrow.

She told me that she would put up with a lot living with other people because the worst thing of all is having to live with yourself.

She used to stay in bed for most of the day & read & drink cups of tea & eat whole packets of biscuits, dunking them in the tea. At night she would put on a huge comfy woollen poncho & go out with Patrick to the Outpost Inn where he would play guitar. I'll tell you about The Outpost Inn later — it's another place that is now buried under the buildings in Collins Street. But I wanted to tell you her comment about her poncho — that it came from somewhere in South America & —

You know the story — it cost 10c at the top of the mountain & $10 at the bottom of the mountain & $100 when it got here, she said.

I think that's a pretty good description of capitalism.

One day when I was waiting at the flat for her to come home someone knocked on the door & I ran downstairs to open it. There were two men standing there. They asked to speak with Karen & I told them she wasn't home. They asked who I was & I said I was a friend of hers.

They said —

You tell Karen that unless the rent she owes us is in our office tomorrow morning we will come around here & dump all her belongings on the footpath.

I started to laugh. I had not had any encounters with people like this or real estate agents & I thought their manner & attitude was theatrical.

We are not joking, one of them said —

we will dump all her furniture — everything — if we do not get the rent money.

Later, when I met her, I told her about this encounter, she sat smoking & thinking & was annoyed with me for laughing. I got the blame for the situation for years after — because I had laughed at the real estate agents. I was meant to not laugh & to negotiate with them.

The blame lasted for ages until finally Patsy said —

Yeah — the situation was because Elaine laughed — not because we were months behind in the rent. Karen stopped trying to blame me after that.

That was when I got involved in their midnight flit. I got the expression from a guy at work when I turned up so very late & he said —

O my — you were involved in a midnight flit & laughed.

We just grabbed everything we could from the flat & took it to a house in Carlton where two friends lived. Karen & Patsy lived with them & slept on their lounge room floor for ages. They were Danny & Daniele. They were very kind people. I haven't seen Danny for ages — I think he went back to Canberra — but I still see Daniele around.

Daniele was always very artistic & she had two sisters. One of them worked at Jimmy Watson's in Carlton & we would go & see her & once she gave us a free feed.

Daniele's mum lived in the Carlton commission flats for a long time — before they moved her to a little cottage in North Carlton. Daniele's family were Italian but had lived in Switzerland for a short time. Their mum lived a very long life. She was a very loveable woman. She was in pain for ages with arthritis in her hip & then when she got a hip replacement she would dance about with joy — showing us the wonders of her new hip.

My favourite story about her is — for years she had a boyfriend who was married & when he died Daniele's mum & the guy's wife comforted one another at his funeral.

I've never heard of that before or since.

Daniele had a story about how horrified her mum was at arriving in Australia & finding that there were no bidets. *People are walking around with shitty bums!* her mum said.

Danny (Daniele's boyfriend) bought an old jaguar because he always wanted a jaguar.

He quickly learned why poor people can buy such a prestigious car cheap. They are notorious for breaking down & costing a fortune to fix.

There's a picture of Karen lying across the bonnet of the jaguar like a parody of a car ad.

She is beaming. I heard that Danny got so fed up with the car that in the end he took it & dumped it in the desert.

There are photographs of me & Karen in the Ivanhoe flat. I would go & talk to her about books & everything. I remember telling her, when I was heartbroken about a bloke, that I could not stand the pain of it & that if it ever happened again I would kill myself.

I was eighteen.

She just listened.

Before I got involved with this guy I fessed up to her that I was in love with him.

Are you in love with him or do you just want to fuck him? She asked.

What's the difference? I asked.

They're both on different plains, she said & took a drag of her cigarette.

She was always funny peculiar about blokes. When she knew I was mad keen on this guy she went to him & asked him if he wanted to fuck. He turned her down. She blamed me & said I must have said something negative to him about her.

There were very few guys I liked but if she ever got to know about it & she knew them too she would always try to 'seduce' them.

Quite often she was successful & managed to spoil any attraction that was developing.

She would report back. One guy she rang up & asked if he wanted to fuck & he said no & so then she said —

How about a blow job then? He did not turn that down. She went around to his house & they had sex. But the minute it was over he jumped out of bed & said that they should not have done it & — would he catch anything? The strange thing about this guy is that he refused to speak to either me or Karen again. It was as if he thought I was involved.

It's pure genius the way a guy like that will do something & then try to make out that it's your fault. But Karen miscalculated — she seemed to think I would be upset & she had enormous confidence that, despite his reaction after they first had sex, she was going to turn him into a toy boy.

I think I will have him as my toy boy, she said when we were sitting having coffee one day & she looked me in the eye as if to challenge me to say something.

It's difficult sometimes in these situations *not* to get annoyed even if your feelings for the person have long died. But all I could think was — where do you get the confidence you will be able to do that?

Her motivations in doing this stuff with men — sabotaging attractions — who knows why — but I think, in part, she wanted to expose the bullshit of things, if there was any bullshit to be found.

Once she told me about a conversation she had with Karina & telling Karina that the boyf that she really fancied was a cook —

Marry him! Said Karina — meaning that this bloke has a sensible & useful job — settle down! Take him up! I was amazed that Karen thought she was able to do this. She always had a lot more faith in these things than me.

That was one of the worst 'love' affairs she ever had. The worst in that I had not seen her as distressed & confused & in that amount of pain. She wandered around my kitchen saying —

I don't get it, I don't get it, we get on, our children get on, why is he disinterested?

She was a lot more forgiving of the blokes than me — if it ended with these guys she was still very nice to them whereas when men have hurt me I usually want nothing to do with them ever again.

But with this guy he told her, a while after their affair was over, how much he valued her friendship & that she *had him for life*. She was happy with this & said it was *all she ever wanted* from him.

But it wasn't at the time. She also told me that she loved his baby's arm. Their routine was he would come & see her & ask advice about his worries — worries about his child or worries about his health & she would give him sensible advice & then they'd fuck.

She tried to talk to him about how much she cared for him but he wasn't interested & said love was 'corny' & suggested she wasn't the kind of woman he was likely to develop those kinds of feelings for. I asked her what that meant & she said — *I am not pretty.*

She thought he had some wit & cleverness but then became disillusioned when she discovered that some of his best lines had been lifted from songs that she heard later.

I think I would have forgiven him everything but when he said to her that it was amazing how clever & funny (funny ha ha) both me & Patsy were — *funny in our souls* — & implied that she wasn't — I was shocked by his blindness to her cleverness & wit.

Later, when we were working with the biddies, (tell you about the biddies later), Karen was in love with the 'The Grey Man.' He had been working as a bar man in a pub (among other jobs) & was married with kids but the kids were grown. He was a lot older than us — maybe 20

years older. He was called the Grey Man because he wore grey clothes &
perhaps because deep down Karen knew he was neither here nor there.
I didn't know what I thought about him until I had a nightmare about
him & told her that I thought he was tyrannical. She denied it. But
another mutual friend of ours thought the same thing. How Karen &
this guy got together was he told her one day in the pub that he loved
her.

I don't know why Karen but I just love you, he said.

She was delighted because she already had a crush on him. He left
his wife & they started planning their future together. I think this one
went for about 2 years & he helped her spend her inheritance from her
mum on restaurants & hotels & holidays.

Point blank she asked for my blessing on this association but I
couldn't give it to her.

I didn't know what to say. I did not feel it to be real & when she said
to me that he had declared his undying love I asked her if she believed
him. She spoke to me as if I had no understanding of such things & said
in a haughty, worldly tone as if she were talking to a child —

Well yes *Elaine I* do. (It's one of the things that makes me miss her
so much — remembering that if she was reading this she would laugh).

Then one morning he woke up & said that he didn't love her
anymore. When she told me this, despite my thoughts, or rather, lack
of thoughts & feelings about him, I was bewildered.

What do you mean? I asked her.

She looked startled & hurt & just shook her head —

He just woke up & said that any love he had — had gone, she said.

It was terrible for her for a long time trying to recover from that
one.

Where he is now I don't know. I guess he'll be really old & I won't
be going looking for him. I'm not sure if anyone tried to find him to tell
him she had died.

I rang another one of her fucks, another one that she had loved, & he said —

Well, you are the third person today who has rung me about this.

He didn't come to her funeral. The story about him was that she told him she loved him & then 'wanted to sink into the floor' because he told her that he 'respected that.' She was never mean about these guys. She left that to me.

It's a dreadful thing to watch a person you are close to & who is deeply hurt because of very many disappointments, abuses & failures go from one bloke to another searching for comfort & connection only to find another shallow moron.

She never thought she would live very long & perhaps she wanted to grab every opportunity. She used to say that she could go into a room & there would be a light over the head of a guy in the room & he would be the one she was attracted to & he would be the one who would give her a hard time.

Once a guy from the Outpost Inn — an interesting person a lot older than me & one of the performers — started asking me out for coffee dates. He was interesting as a performer but not as a boyfriend. I went out with him once. I would have been about 19 or 20.

His conversation was ridiculous & patronising & actually more of a lecture on the world & what was going on in it. I sat & listened, irritated & bored, & marvelling at the fantasy he was living out in front of me. After he had said his piece & decided that the coffee date was over he got up to leave. I was astonished that I had not been given any chance to speak or reply & started to argue with him.

A few days later Karen & Patsy came around to my flat & Karen said —

Don't get involved with this guy — he will really hurt you. She really hated him & claimed it was because he had badly hurt Mad Margaret (will tell you about Mad Margaret soon).

Karen freaked me out with her vehemence about *not* going out with him. But it didn't really matter to me one way or another because I wasn't interested.

When I went back to the Outpost Inn he started asking me out again & I said I didn't want to go.

Come over here, he said — *don't think of anything else — just think about you & me,* he said — *one to one, person to person* & he gestured back & forward from himself to me & back again.

No, I don't want to go again, I said.

He said — *I noticed that when we stopped talking the other night you suddenly started to argue with me at the end of our conversation. I took that to mean that you didn't want our meeting to end & to leave & you were really trying to keep the conversation going.*

No that was not it, I said. I didn't bother to explain. Then he went & told another bloke from the group, who regularly went to the Inn, that I was totally under the spell of Karen & whatever Karen told to me to do I would do. This friend laughed & said —

So he had it totally right — he was onto everything!

I didn't bother to put any of them straight — that the truth was I did not like this man & didn't want to spend any more time with him. I just let them go ahead & think Karen was the boss of me. They would never have believed me anyway. Goodness knows that was probably what Karen thought too.

The Outpost Inn was a place where musicians came to perform. We had to go down these stairs into an underground sort of place. It was in Collins Street. The same crowd went there regularly. There was a big guy who ran it & he served snacks. I don't think there was any alcohol but we were kids anyway when we first went. I think we went there on & off from when we were about 16 until we were about 19. I met someone recently who said that it was set up by Christian minded people who wanted to provide a place for young people to go & perform & watch other people perform. Danny, who I mentioned above with the jaguar, he would play guitar & he absolutely worshipped David Bowie. He was always playing Ziggy when he got onstage. I don't know when it opened or when it closed but it was one of the more fun places to go as a teenager.

On countless occasions when I went around to see her in the Ivanhoe flat we would talk about books. I was reading Thomas Hardy novels for English classes at school & she started slagging him off.

Thomas Hardy is boring, she said — *And he compares people to buildings.*

She got annoyed with me for defending him & later she challenged me for giving her attitude about Thomas Hardy. I said that she might at least have read him.

I have read him, she said. But I wasn't sure that was true. Hardly anyone reads books — they read the critics.

Sometimes the critics haven't read the books!

I bought a book by Ernest Hemingway once & it was second-hand & had a newspaper article in it that was a critical review of the book. I read the review after I read the book & it was slagging off Hemingway for bragging about his time in the trenches during a war. That didn't happen in the book! He took the piss out of people trying to reward him for bravery in the trenches. When they said to him something like —

We are giving you an award for your bravery when a grenade went off in the trench. He said — *I was eating a piece of cheese.*

Maybe that's why the person who sold the book added the newspaper cutting.

Because it was a bullshit review.

It must have been awful for her after she left school. My friends & I had worked really hard & did well at HSC. At the time the results came out I had gone to a friend's house who I had studied with. There were a group of us there & we were all really happy because we had all done well & were likely to get into our various courses at uni. She must have rung my aunt's house, where I was living, looking for me & then got the phone number of my friend & rang me there.

What did you get? She asked & I don't remember if she congratulated me. Maybe — but she didn't sound pleased or happy because she would have been able to do anything she liked but couldn't. For years afterwards she would say — *Some of the best minds in the country have never done HSC.* Which is certainly true.

Mad Margaret

Margaret was a lot older than us & she was an artist — she painted fabulous colourful oil paintings. I can't remember much about them, but I have a landscape painting of hers.

It is a scene of High Street in Northcote but you would not be able to recognise the street.

The painting has buildings made of brick & a little 1960's style car going down the road & a beautiful old light & tree branches overhanging the street. It is done in many different colours.

I had a job when I was 19 & I asked her if I could buy this painting & offered her $50 — which was not a bad offer back then — it was about half my weekly wage or an entire week of the dole or nearly two weeks rent. It is a tiny little painting not much bigger than A4 size. She was always complaining about not having money. She was so happy & couldn't believe it when I offered & I gave her the money & took the painting &, despite every move in all the houses I've lived in over the years, I still have it.

When I was at uni I wanted to write an essay about her. I went to one of the teachers in the Art History department & asked if I could but they wanted to know why. I said that I really liked her & all the artists we were asked to write about were men.

Can't men create great art? asked the teacher.

We don't know who she is, she said. They wouldn't allow it.

I think the university is a museum that deals in dead ideas. It is a corporation but one that the government can control. It's a business where you are discouraged from creativity & passion. You must write on the subjects they want you to write about &, more importantly, in the structure that they want it. Perhaps because the academics are often overworked & they mark on a rubric & need to tick the boxes in 15 minutes. The university has become more conservative over the years.

Can't men create great art is a wonderful line though. I've had a lot of laughs with people about it.

Karen described Margaret as the person who came to her mind when reading the line from Ginsberg — *I saw the best minds of my generation destroyed by madness.* Karen was filled with sorrow & regret when she said this to me. For a long time I thought Ginsberg's poem was expressing this too — expressing sorrow & regret — but Forbes, the poetry teacher, said no — that Ginsberg, in *Howl*, is *celebrating* the life of these people.

I felt embarrassed when Forbes pointed this out to me because I thought I had missed the point of the poem but there was no discussion — he just told me the meaning of the poem. Now I don't think it is that straight forward at all.

Karen loved it when I repeated back to her conversations I heard her having with Margaret —

Margaret: (in raspy desperate tones, dragging on cigarettes) *Do you think he really loves me Karen?*

Karen: (Dragging on cigarette & thinking & nodding) *Yes I do Margaret, I really do.*

Margaret: *Do you really? You think he loves me? You really think so? Why do you think that?*

Karen: *Because he treats you differently to the way he treats everybody else.*

Karen would kill herself laughing when I repeated this back to her. She always tried hard to comfort people & to tell them what they wanted to hear. Margaret was the one who got hurt by the guy at the Outpost who tried to go out with me.

Sometimes Margaret would get stressed about the police. There was a café in Faraday Street Carlton — Genevieve's — & Margaret saw this place as a sanctuary for bohemians like herself. But one night the cops came through the place. I don't know much more about the story

— what the cops were looking for or anything — but Margaret saw this as a sign that we were moving towards a police state.

Margaret: *Can you believe Karen — that the cops came into Genevieve's — Genevieve's! What are these cats doing coming in there? This is not right! What is happening? These cats coming into Genevieve's.*

Karen: (Nodding) *Yes, I know it's terrible, terrible.*

Margaret: *But these cats walked in — took over — into Genevieve's!*

Karen: *Yes, I know, it's outrageous.*

When Margaret was with Karen she would stare at her as if Karen could anchor her to the world and make her feel safe and calm.

Margaret would sometimes have me come over & stay with her in her house in Kew.

I think it was a house she got out of her disastrous marriage. She had some beautiful children who were bright & sane & her little boy was often exasperated with his mother.

She had troubles with her family — her parents & uncles & the like — I don't think they approved of her and I think they had her sent to the psych wards. I am not sure what treachery happened there. I never met any of them but Margaret told me that sometimes they would try & buy back her affections by doing things for her like buying her a new fridge.

She said that she would accept their kind offers & take whatever they gave her but it made no difference to how she felt about them. I think it was the first time I had heard someone being honest about how to play people who try to buy you. I also think I remember it because that strategy wouldn't work for me. I would feel that there was a price to be paid somehow. If I really wanted nothing to do with people — better to have *nothing* to do with them.

One of the best times I had with Margaret was when we were at the Universal Workshop & a guy (who I later found out was the poet PiO) was reading out one of his poems from his collection called *Fuck Poems*. He was yelling — *Cock, Clit, Cock, Clit* — at various volumes &

with various repetitions of these words. Margaret was pretending to be aghast & shocked & appalled at the standard of poetry today.

Well, really, I don't know. Is this poetry? she said.

I wrote to PiO recently to ask if it was him that night — about 40 years ago & he said that it was & that someone had tried to rip off his idea & had written — cock, cunt, cock, cunt... but that was *not* the spirit of the poem at all.

Patsy kept in touch with Margaret &, when she died a few years ago, he attended her funeral. I told him I wished I knew about it & I would have gone. In her later years she had gone back to the religion she had tried to escape. She had a stroke & the doctors tried to get her to recover by doing gentle exercises. They suggested that she begin with just squeezing a ball in her hand to get the circulation going & to strengthen her hand. But she wouldn't do it & said that her life was in the hands of Jesus & that He would look after her. So she died.

Karen & I drifted away from her many years ago but when I sit quietly & remember these unique & desperate people I really appreciate & miss them. And, as I told you, I still have her beautiful painting.

Smoking

It was me who gave Karen her first cigarette. We were on our way to Eaglemont station & I was smoking & I asked her — *do you want one?* And she took it & that was it.

By the end of her life, with her asthma & everything, her doctor said she could hardly breathe. I started smoking when I was about 13.

I didn't do the draw back until I was about 14. I felt sick when I did the drawback, like you do. But I persisted until I was addicted & so then I loved it. I finally gave up when I was about 30. I had stopped many times over the years, for years at a time, but I really gave it away then. I've told people my trick for quitting but I don't know anyone who has tried it & succeeded. My brother tried it & a friend tried it but they only lasted a few weeks. The reason they both went back to smoking was because they thought it was easy to quit & they could just have one. But no. You have to take it in how addictive it is & you have to take it in that you can't have one.

It was 30 years ago that I quit & because I associate smoking with my youth & going out with people & being thin — because I reckon they lie about how much weight you pile on — I sometimes think of having one. But I can't because I want to live. But here's what I did to quit. I stayed up late & smoked all the fags in the packet & told myself that I'd eat whatever I wanted & drink as much coffee as I wanted & deal with those problems another time because the smoking was the problem. There were two ideas that I had that helped me to give up. One was that I figured if I had the internal dialogue — *will I? won't I? will I? won't I?* — I would *always* find a reason to give in & have one. How can you fight an addiction with willpower like that? I knew it wouldn't work. I talked myself into believing that I did not smoke & that there was no need to feel tempted because there was going to be no internal talk about it. I blocked the voice that would talk me into it.

The second idea I had was one I read in a magazine. The idea was — once you have developed a serious smoking habit you cannot have just one. You will resume your habit. I found that really helpful. It took two goes for me to quit. The first time I quit for two years & the second time I quit for good. Well, for the last 30 years. I had a puff of a cigar on my brother's 50 birthday & was obsessed again with smoking for about two weeks. That's how addicted to it I am. I had to talk myself out of going to the tobacconist in Flinders Street every time I passed it.

But anyway just thought I'd tell you about that before I tell you about how much we smoked & how much we loved it. Karen discovered the lovely Sobranies — glorious pastel-coloured cigarettes with gold paper around the filter. And the lovely Gitanes in the blue packet with art work that looks like a Matisse cut out. We tried pouch tobacco — Drum & Bank & Port Royal. The Indonesian cigarettes that smell of cloves started off very nicely but then quickly got too much. The Universal Workshop in Fitzroy where we used to hang out in our late teens reeked of them. We smoked Winfield, Viscount, Peter Stuyvesant (I smoked these with my grandmother —but they were full on), Rothmans, Marlboro, Woodbine, Alpine (smoked these for a while with my one & only girlfriend) & perhaps others I have forgotten. With the Viscounts you could get a packet of 10 for about 40c & so, for $1, you could go to the city on the train, get a packet of fags, wander around, get a cappuccino & come home. Like I told you about that before.

The thing about smoking is that it was great fun exploring & trying all the brands but then in the end you settle down to one brand & just keep smoking because you are hooked & it has no interest in it anymore — it's just a thing you do. But it was great fun to catch taxis, called cabs back then, & smoke sobranies & go to hotels/pubs in the city.

One night we were in a really daggy hotel the Southern Cross — one they've pulled down now — & we were eating spaghetti bolognese

& drinking & I was helping Karen to put in an application to go to La Trobe Uni.

La Trobe were always giving people a chance who hadn't gone through the usual routes to uni. She had to write an essay on a topic they gave her & she had to put in a personal essay — explaining why she wanted to go to uni — & she asked me to go over it with her. I can't remember anything about the essay on a topic, I don't think she showed that to me, but the personal essay was very funny where she compared herself to Eliza Doolittle from *Pygmalion* because of her apprenticeship in floristry.

That was the first time I saw Karen really frightened & underconfident about her abilities. I told her the essay was really great — hilarious & witty & I was astonished at her shyness. I tried to make her feel that her abilities were beyond question & not to entertain any doubt. They did offer her a place at the uni. She started studying things like linguistics and the French Revolution. This was great because I was also studying the French Revolution — the 1789 one. We loved Georges Lefebvre & the way he talked about the people in the revolution. I also loved Olwen Hufton. She did a lot of detailed work. She was very cautious & careful. The words the historians used about the revolution showed what they thought about people — whether they were a mob or 'the people' or a crowd. Karen loved that Lefebvre had compassion. I always had trouble with history & politics because I worried about them executing people. Hardly anyone ever worries about this. They don't get stuck on people being executed. They don't care about the royals getting shot — like the Romanovs or Marie Antoinette or her hubby getting their heads chopped off. They don't care that Che Guevara oversaw the execution of people imprisoned in Cuba. They shrug & say — *o well* — *everybody is involved with these things in such times.* And I say — *o well* — *this is not revolutionary.*

Pubs

When we were in our late teens & Karen had moved to Carlton she liked to go to the Fitzroy pubs. I didn't get it. I wasn't interested in drinking & I didn't understand her interest in the people in the pubs who she worshipped & adored. A lot of them were quite a bit older than us. Some were from the Sydney Push &, even in much later years, she was bedazzled that one of its members took a romantic interest in her. But I never liked the men in these pubs — never liked their macho posturing. In fact — I had never seen anything like it.

Everything about these men appalled me. The way they leaned on the bar. Their authoritative way of speaking. The way they would assume we were morons & hold forth on every topic under the sun. One time a guy said to me that the prints on the wall of a pub were by an artist called Margaret Preston — *but that's art & you wouldn't know anything about that.*

The prints were not by Margaret Preston.

One time a guy kept feeling my leg & saying to the table of people — *I don't know why you can't just say you want a root when you want a root.*

I want my baby back, he said. He was depressed because his girlfriend had dumped him.

What's going on with your girlfriend? Asked Karen.
She said I had to pick between her & alcohol, he said.
It looks like you've made your choice, said Karen.
After a little while he vomited in his lap —
Your friend has vomited in his lap, I said to his pal.
His pal looked at me in disgust as if *I* was the one who was uncool to draw attention to this.

The one that Karen was flattered by ended up hitting her. She had to get out of it. She was more in love with another guy — the one with a dick the size of a baby's arm. This line about a guy having *a dick the size of a baby's arm* we loved & used so often that one day when we saw an ad on telly with a baby's arm we burst out laughing.

But the horror story about this Push guy was he got really ratty when he seemed to come to believe that she would be the last woman to fall for him. That's what Karen thought was going on. Who knows — maybe it was true. When she ended it he kept hounding her for money he claimed she owed him. She saw him again a few years later in one of the Fitzroy pubs & she had money from her mother's estate so she took out her cheque book & wrote him a cheque. She thought it was mean to do this because it brought it to an end & he knew it.

He saw me once in Brunswick Street & I tried to say hello to him & he kept staring at me with eyes full of cold rage & fear & hate. But, at the same time, desperation.

I had nothing to do with it. I only heard the stories. It's one of the spookiest things I have seen — the ambivalence in the eyes of these men. I had one boyfriend that I met in a café, not long before he died, & even though he was falling apart physically, he looked at me with a sickening expression— it said — *please feel sorry for me I am appealing to your compassion, kindness & softness — but this will not stop me attacking you & trying to dominate you.*

He was my domesticated violence story. Karen & I always thought the expression 'domestic violence' was a joke. Like domestic violence did not count as violence. Some people think it doesn't.

There was a young woman in one of these pubs that we were friends with. She was a delightful person. The men kept telling us that she was stupid. I don't know why. Perhaps because she unashamedly liked sex & would take the men home — particularly one or both of two brothers who Karen nicknamed The Sleaze Brothers.

Because the men were so awful about her we kept trying to 'radicalise' her by giving her books like *The Second Sex*. She would absolutely kill herself laughing & say —

Why do you guys keep giving me feminist books? She was younger than us by a few years but much more together in many ways. She lived in a group house in Fitzroy with people much older than her who adored her. She ended up going to Canberra & I heard she became a madam in a brothel. I would love to meet her again. It makes me sad to think I won't see again some of the people that Karen led me to.

We used to go back & forward from the pubs to the Universal Workshop. The Universal Workshop was called the Universal Wankshop by some. I do like Alexei Sayle's line about the word 'workshop' — any person who uses the word, unless they are referring to light engineering, is a twat.

But we loved the Universal Workshop. It was a huge factory building that went for nearly a whole block in Fitzroy. There's a Naturopathy school there now. Back in the 1970's it was full of café's & spaces for talks & exhibitions & shops with hippy clothes & incense. You could see poetry & music performances. I think money won in the end. Despite all the hippy vibe I don't think it made enough money & got sold on or rented out or whatever.

I would go to the University & do stuff there & then come down to Fitzroy to the pubs to meet her & we'd often move on to the Workshop.

There would be confusing things happen at the Uni & I would run them by her.

Once I saw a young woman putting up posters for their Zionist club. I didn't know anything about this & had a vague understanding that it had something to do with Jewish people. I asked this young woman about it & went around with her at the campus helping her put up the posters & talking to her about it.

I can't remember a single thing she said but she kept introducing me to her friends saying — *I couldn't get anyone to help me put up the posters & so, here I am! I've got my non-Jewish friend to help me.*

She kept saying this again & again. When I got to the pub to meet up with Karen I told her the story & said —

But you know the strange thing is — she never asked me if I was Jewish.

Karen laughed & shook her head & said — *It's nothing but a boring racist little game.*

You have no idea how many people I've told this story to — in order to show how Karen knew about these things more than I did. She had been busily getting herself an education. But the reaction of lots of people was — *But you don't look Jewish.*

I still think this comment is very bizarre coming from people who claim to be all lefty liberals. What does a Jewish person look like?

But K did meet at least one interesting & very nice man at the pubs. His name is Tim. He is Christopher's father. Christopher is Karen's first son. Tim is an artist & I have one of his artworks on my wall called *Elephant Ears*. It shows him & Christopher walking across the Hoddle Street Bridge (when Chris was a little boy) & Tim is throwing a football into the air. It's a black & white print & it's called Elephant Ears because he's given himself & Chris one huge ear each.

University

Karen was impressed with one of the academics we met at uni & this academic used to hang around with us quite a bit & would say she was *picking our brains for all our little ideas* — mainly about feminism which was new to her but we had been reading about it since we were around 15. Some women were coming to understand that feminism had currency & you could start to make a career out of it. I mention this person because she brought about one of the strangest incidents that happened between me & Karen. The awful truth is that we were impressed by the teacher because she was highly qualified & was very good at exams & we thought for sure she must be clever. Maybe she is, maybe she isn't, but we were way too old (in our early 20's) to be believing that for those reasons. We started to lose our bedazzlement because often, when she couldn't understand some of the ideas we were discussing, she would become kind of aggressive & say — *I don't get it!*

We would be chatting away about all the things we had read & we would be excited about all the ideas we were discovering & she would say — *I don't get it!* Like it was our fault, that we were being idealistic or poetic or illogical or impractical in some way. Anyway, I got sick of her picking my brains 'for all your little ideas' for which I would rarely get credit & I was very depressed about everything to do with uni & feminism so one day I told her that I felt very paranoid but that all this brain picking stuff was wrong & I didn't want to do it anymore. She was angry & said — *You are right. You are paranoid!* But, deep down, I could tell from her outraged 'rabbit in the headlights' look that she knew it was true. She went to Karen to tell Karen how crazy I was & how outrageous were my complaints about the immorality of her taking credit for things. Karen rang me & said the whole conversation had made her feel completely schitzy (crazy) because she had already thought word for word everything that I was reported to have said but neither of us had had a discussion about this & so it confused her

70

how we could have *exactly* the same ideas & use exactly the same words when we had thought them but had not spoken them.

Carson McCullers writes of love as a one-way street. It is very rare for her to mention the mutuality of it. There is a couple in *The Heart is a Lonely Hunter* who had fought &, after the fight, had never gone back to addressing one another the same way. But she writes of how there was genuine love between them. But in *The Ballad of the Sad Café* she writes of the 'curt truth' that the beloved hates & fears the lover.

But friendship is not sexual love.

In *The Bridge of San Luis Rey* Thornton Wider says of his character Doña Micaela Villegas

— *she had never realized any love save love as passion. Such love, though it expends itself in generosity and thoughtfulness, though it give birth to visions and to great poetry, remains among the sharpest expressions of self-interest.... Many who have spent a lifetime in it can tell us less of love than the child that lost a dog yesterday.*

I think of this last line often. Even though my friendship with Karen was not 'love as passion' in the sense that he means it, I worry that I can tell you less of love than 'the child that lost a dog yesterday'. And then I think there is no reason to believe that the child is not eloquent about the dog who died & perhaps the child will speak in poetry & that dogs are more intelligent than we think & the love we have for them is a good thing.

There were very few things that I was introduced to at uni that were exciting. Usually I unearth these things for myself or had them introduced to me by friends like Karen.

Lots of times when people find that you have an interest in a subject they automatically think that you studied it at uni. Nope. When I read *The Bridge of San Luis Rey* it was in a hardback volume of short novels & when I finished the story, I wondered how I could not have known of Thornton Wilder. This was before the internet & because the book of novels was a hardback book with a plain cover it was not covered in puffs like are all over paperback books. I rang my brother & asked him if he could go to the Black Mask bookshop in South Yarra on his way home from work & ask them about Thornton Wilder & while I waited I thought — *if no one has heard of this writer there is no justice in the world.* But Wilder was famous & had been for decades.

Although Karen & I often shared the same passions for certain ideas sometimes I would become obsessed with the brilliance of a thing & focus on it. I read Kafka's *The Castle* over & over & also Genet's *Miracle of the Rose.* It's strange that when a book is truly mysteriously brilliant then I cannot remember the incidents in it & it seems new to me when I reread it. I do remember that they were hunting escaped children with pitchforks in *Miracle of the Rose* & they murdered Harcamone & the intricate detail Genet goes into explaining emotions & these emotions are conveyed & created with simple gestures — like, for example, small dismissive movements of the hand to convey to his beloved that he is less full of passion than he really is. Some books create such strong passions in me that I cannot read them again. Like *The Border Trilogy* by Cormack McCarthy.

The one thing I do remember being excited about at uni was some of the film directors.

It is impossible to explain the joy that Jean-Luc Godard movies brought. Pierrot Le Fou, Breathless, *À bout de soufflé* Wind from the East, *Le Vent d'est.* We saw a lot of amazing films at uni. Like *Battleship Potemkin* & *Bicycle Thieves.* I hate watching movies more than once but I watched Godard movies for the feeling he created — that entirely new ways of expressing yourself are possible.

Karen was an extra in a film — *Where the Green Ants Dream.* You can see her in the courtroom scene with a shock of bleached blonde hair. She talked to me about how sensitive Herzog was in the way he interacted with the aboriginal people in the film.

He was reeeeaaaally slick, she said.

Once when I went around to Karen's place in North Carlton she sat & read Kafka's *Metamorphosis* out loud from beginning to end. When she began with the opening sentence I kept saying — *it does not say that!?*

It does, she said.

It does not say that, I said & kept laughing.

It does, she said & kept reading. I had never heard anything like it.

When I finished at uni I was very depressed. I was depressed for many reasons but one of them was because I felt we were never going to make any changes, particularly regarding women. It was a losing battle & part of the reason was because a lot of the women we were involved with were careerists who could see that 'feminism' was a currency they could use to promote their career. But Karen had some detachment from it all.

We're never going to win, I said.

You stopped, she said — *And that's why reality hit you. We'll do it differently next time.*

Feminism

We had been interested in feminism or Women's Liberation since we were very young.

We knew the game was rigged. Karen told me that calling it 'women's lib' was uncool (when I was about 20) & I should call it feminism.

We were only involved with it for a few years but it seems like 100 because we started reading books about it when we were in our late teens & started to go to feminist meetings & conferences & women's dances when we were in our early 20's. For me I was over it almost overnight when I was 24. I had (what I felt were) a series of epiphanies — like the one described above about 'never winning' — & went on to other problems. Most of it is pretty boring but I'll tell you some of the great fun we had with things that I guess could be described as 'feminist.' I agree with Fran Lebovitz — women don't get to say whether they are feminist or not — you can try & claim you are or you aren't but — like gentiles often decide who's Jewish — other people decide if you are feminist or not.

I stood in front of a friend of my mum's when I was 16 & said — *No, I don't think you should take a man's name when you marry.* She looked at me with amazement & horror & said — *But* — that's *women's lib!*

We read most of the famous tomes, but I could never read Kate Millett's book. We loved Germaine Greer who we called Germs & sat in Karen's mum's flat watching the Greer interview where, leaning against a brick wall, she looks up & says — *Australia God damn!*

I always thought she was a very unique person who defied a label & marveled at the way she could make claims about the world & have the confidence to make these claims when the world seemed to be too full of information to be able to make claims about it.

Several women I knew had tried to use an IUD as a form of contraception & it had failed for various reasons. Karen used hers as an earring. I'm not sure people would know what it was.

We also developed a certain defiance about the taboo of menstrual blood. But the reactions were quite boring — I had been swimming at a friend's place & had blood on the back of my school uniform. I left it there & didn't change. A friend of my aunt's took me aside & told me confidentially, woman to woman, as if I'd have a fit, in a conspiratorial whisper that — *There's blood on the back of your school dress you know.*

I lost my nerve & just said — *Yes, — thanks.*

But of all the tomes & all the pranks we loved Valerie Solanas & her *Scum Manifesto* the most & it stayed with us.

We first found Valerie (that's what we called her) when we were about 22. The story went around that her book was found in a remainder bin in Coles along with a whole load of Mills & Boon. It could be true — it was certainly considered rubbish & throw-away by many.

Nearly every line from Valerie was & is quotable. But people focus on the hilarious descriptions & put-downs of men & ignore lines that go under her wall of rage & hate.

Lines like — *the only wrong is to hurt others, and the meaning of life is love.*

But mostly Karen & I loved her for the extreme black comedy. We quoted the lines again & again & never tired of them. By the time we got up to Valerie I had had enough of feminism. Of studying it & reading about it I mean. Feminist books are very negative. I felt overwhelmed with the sadness of it. It was too much for me & I needed positive & constructive ways to look at the world.

Valerie was a lot of fun but I don't think she was joking.

Heroin

I don't know when Karen & I stopped talking about ideas. The last few times I saw her she was drugged or wanting to be. After her mother died, we used to go to Northlands & wander around. We'd eat daggy food like those 6-point sandwiches where one is egg & one is corned beef with pickle — those sandwiches cut into triangles & wrapped tightly in plastic wrap. Then we'd drink cappuccinos because they are daggy & comforting. Karen was in grief.

This was before she had the distraction of The Grey Man.

She had come into quite a bit of Marie's money & she told me that she was able to buy some very nice heroin.

O Elaine, you don't know what it's like, she said — *to know that I could take a drug & not feel any of this.*

I didn't understand her comment.

Don't you even want to feel your own mother's death? I thought & — *Is that moral?*

She said that when you lose a lover the pain is very intense — but to lose your mum is a much deeper pain. Now you have to cut it on your own.

At her funeral Christopher said that Karen's loss of her mum was a loss that she just could not get over.

When we worked in the biddie home together there was a woman who worked there who was much older than us who made a meal of pain & sorrow. We called her 'Dearly Loved, Sadly Missed.' One day she said to me —

Some people's lives are destroyed by grief Elaine.

I tried to imagine it. I was thirty & could not imagine it.

There was a biddie, in the home who had varicose ulcers & she would have her legs regularly cleaned & treated & bound with bandages. She would shuffle around.

Dearly Loved, Sadly Missed told me that the ulcers the old woman had would have been extremely painful but you could see for yourself, in her face, the physical pain she was in. Despite this she was a very good-natured person & the only times she would get angry & upset was when the medical staff persisted in torturing her. There were drugs to help her with the pain in her legs but they would ration them & the pain was rarely properly controlled. Their excuse for not controlling it was their concern about her becoming 'addicted' to the drugs for the pain — or that the drugs would affect her health. Not much thought went into this — she was as old as god's dog. I think the medical staff were on auto pilot.

Sometimes she would become exasperated & say —

It's my *pain not* their *pain. O, I shouldn't take it out on you dear.*

The old woman had a son & he had died of an asthma attack. She talked to me about how he had been married but his wife had become disinterested in married life & wanted to leave & continue going out & partying. She described the terrible sorrow her son experienced & how she had to support & comfort him.

Then, not long after, he died.

I would go in to see her in her little 'independent living' bedsit room. She would have just had her legs cleaned & dressed & bandaged. She would be lying on her bed curled up & she would be cuddling a photograph, still in its frame, of her son.

Karen acquired a taste for heroin in her early 20's & stopped for a while when she had Polly.

It was a very boring drug to be around but she told me that the rush when you took it was more intense than orgasm — because it took you more out of yourself — you could think of nothing else. She also said that the thought of living without it & never having it again was too sad.

Many times she tried to quit — I went with her to a clinic in North Melbourne where they make you take a substance to see if you are really addicted to heroin before they put you on the methadone program. They give you this stuff & see if you react to it & feel sick. I thought this was crazy and brutal. She was scared & nervous. But she 'passed' by getting sick & was duly provided with the methadone. I saw her, after some time when we took a break, when we had had a fight, walking down Queens Parade in Clifton Hill with her usual book in her hand. I think I was sitting with my brother drinking coffee & she came by. She sat with us & immediately we all began to laugh at various things. Sometimes she would look me in the eye. She seemed in good spirits. She seemed like her usual irreverent, treasonous, heretical self.

I am not sure how long she stayed using just the methadone but in one of the last meetings I had with her I was about 40 or 41 & she said in a dreamy, distracted way — *When are you going to have a baby? It's now or never for you isn't it? I think it is really sad if you don't have a baby because I always thought you'd make a great mum.*

I don't know why she said this. Whether she genuinely believed this or whether she was just seeing if she could get a reaction.

Not the old 'sad' routine, I said.

She was shocked that I stood up to her.

How am I supposed to have a baby when I have no husband or partner?

Don't worry about that, she said.

You want me living on a pension in a commission flat? I said.

It was like she was turning into a different person with ordinary ideas. But living in poverty in a commission flat was what she was doing & I suppose it was another way she wanted to take me with her.

Depression

When she first started to use heroin we were in our early 20's.

I had just finished at uni & was lost & seriously depressed. I couldn't eat & couldn't sleep & would get out of bed to vomit if I was able to get out of bed. She was loyal & supportive to me. I kept saying to her —

I feel it in my heart, there is a massive, blasted hole in my chest.

Just be around people that you trust, she said.

I asked her about the time when we were kids at school — did she feel it in her chest?

She said no— she felt the pain in her stomach. I couldn't be around people who would say anything harsh to me because it would all go straight into the hole in my chest.

She said when she felt like that, when we were young, she was afraid of me. Afraid of my sarcasm or meanness. One day, as I was sitting staring out into space, still trying to decipher why I felt so bad, someone in the house offered me heroin. They said if I took it would make me *feel a whole lot better.*

I can't do that, I said — *I will never get better.*

They looked at me in surprise. I had an intuition that if I took it whatever was eating my insides would stop & wait & grow bigger & then, when I tried to stop taking it, would come back & kill me.

Maybe it was the lizard that I described to you above.

But, like I said, heroin was quite boring to be around. It was especially boring when I would go with her to pubs & we would be all set to go on a pub crawl around Fitzroy & meet all sorts of fun & interesting people & end up in the 'sly grog' & have conversations with poets like Shelton Lee. But this all stopped when she got involved with heroin because she'd have a few drinks & then want what she described as her 'drug of choice.'

This meant going to the local squat.

The squat was permanently occupied by 2 people, one was an artist & I don't know what her partner did, maybe he was a dealer. Years later I saw her partner a few times in Smith Street. Once he was yelling at a dog tied to a pole —

Don't behave like that with me!

He was very indignant that the dog didn't show him the respect he thought he deserved.

And the second time I talked to him about how Karen had died & he said —

O — not another one! I guess for him all the deaths of overdoses all melded into one & were the same.

I found out recently that he had died of Hep C.

K would take me around to the squat and we'd sit around with the woman of the house — she was a very pleasant innocent kind of person — & all the people dropping in to score — & score for their tricks — but mostly it was quite dull after people had had their shot.

Sometimes they would have interesting conversations. One young woman came there &, after they had taken the heroin & wiped up the blood, they sat & had a chat about Mozart & Debussy & singing & how Polly loved the nun who came to her school because she was a lovely lady with a blue veil. The young woman had to go because she had a trick waiting for his half in the car & the women urged her to sing for the joy of it. I wrote a poem once about this — it was a dreamy conversation. I'll show you the poem in a minute.

Usually, when you go to houses, you look for something cosy or interesting but this house had things that were like *The Amityville Horror.* It wasn't full of lived-in grot or anything like that — it was as if the building was under construction. As if the walls & roof didn't keep the earth out. In winter there was a fire in the fireplace. I could imagine someone leaning over it & looking into the fire & saying — *this is the road to hell.*

Here is the Heroin Poem:

Heroin

Sitting in a café a man with black clothes and tufted hair
   spoke to Karen and told her the way to clean rose quartz beads of
bad vibrations
   is to dunk them in salt water
   (rose quartz beads are good for your heart chakra)
   That's a marvellous black leather jacket I said
   Yes I've had it a long time he said
   He scratched and blinked and off he went
   He was on the nod said Karen

I nearly lost her said Mandy
   Her lips went blue and the white kept spreading
   We threw her in the bath and ran the water and slapped her face
   Don't go don't go we yelled at her Come back
   I don't remember any of it said Kerry
   I only remember sinking and feeling so relaxed

I close my eyes when they stick the needle in
   when it was over and arms were rubbed Karen said
   my little girl is becoming a Catholic
   I asked her why and she said oh but
   the lady comes to school and she is so beautiful
   she wears a long dress and a blue veil
   Children love all of that don't they said Mary
   They think of the angels and heaven and god

I'd like to learn singing said Karen
    I don't know if I have the voice
    I'd be very surprised if you don't said Anna
    I'll find you a good teacher
    Are you still waitressing asked Karen
    I was never waitressing said Anna
    You're a working girl are you said Karen and we laughed

Anna burned the white powder in a teaspoon
    When I opened my eyes there was blood running down her arm
    What music do you like she asked
    Debussy said Karen and Bach
    and Mozart said Anna you have to like Mozart
    I have to go there's a man waiting for the syringe
    We'll go too said Karen
    Next time I'll give you the names of singing teachers said Anna
    but you should just sing
    Just sing for the pure joy of it she said
    and went off into the night

Dream 4/4/2020

Last night I dreamed that Karen was back to life & I was meeting her in a bar. It seemed to be up in Northcote somewhere. Maybe the Peacock Hotel. We had both written something, a small story. I gave her mine to read & she loved it & it made her laugh. But someone in the pub was going on to *her* about what she had written & telling her she should work on it because it was so great. I was furious! I said to her —

Well you go & work on your stuff & good luck to you!

It was like I was leaving her. Then later I came back & I was hugging her & I couldn't believe that she had come back to life.

I have had dreams about people who I have loved who have died & the dreams are often the same — they appear to me & I say —

What are you doing here? You are dead! And they say — *I have had a reprieve!*

It seems perfectly natural in the dream that they have had a reprieve & they have come to visit.

I think this recurring dream might have started because my grandmother kept having reprieves in real life when she was sick & dying with cancer. We would think she was going to die soon & then she would pull through. She was the first person who I loved who died. The strange thing about the dream about Karen is that there was a feeling of her having been dead a long, long time.

I suppose, objectively speaking, she has but it feels like it was only a few years ago. When Ridi died it felt like Karen was dug up.

The other day I saw some images of Frida Kahlo's clothes & her Revlon nail polish & her corsets she used to wear to help support her back & I wondered what people could want from these things that were dusty & old & macabre & saturated with death. Perhaps these thoughts were in my mind when I had the dream about Karen. I felt the truth of her death intensely & that it is unhealthy & macabre to be talking about her. But I do want to tell you about her. It seems to be part of life to tell you about her. Not the same as making fetishes of her belongings.

Spirited Away

About a year after K died I was sitting on my bed with my little nephew & we started to watch *Spirited Away* — the Miyazaki film. My nephew went to sleep but I was hypnotised by the film.

Sen was washing the river spirit & needed two bars of soap to do it. And she had to swim down & pull out a sharp thing that was sticking in him &, with the removal of the object, came all the debris that was trapped in him.

I was transfixed by the psychological truth of the film. Watching it made me realise that something was bothering me. For ages I was in a dream-like state when Karen died but not aware of it. Not long after watching the film I went to get help. When I went to see the psychiatrist I didn't know it was Karen's death that was bothering me. And, when I realised it was, I said to the shrink that I knew why I was so stressed & it was very hard for me to say. He thought that my big burdensome secret was something to do with me as a child & began to talk about going to the police.

No, not me, I said. And I told him about Karen & he said —*So she was like a sister?*

Yes, I said — *Like a sister.*

My first conversation with the psychiatrist might make you laugh.

I always feel nervous before I see psychiatrists because I worry they will think I am a fraud & not really nuts.

But they never do. They seem to see that I am very disturbed about something.

He asked me what I was doing & I told him about the writing.

What have you been reading? he asked.

I've been re-reading Thomas Hardy novels, I said.

Do you think you will write like Thomas Hardy? he asked.

No, I said.

What else are you reading? he asked.

I like the Beats, I said.

You like Jack Kerouac? he asked.

Not so much, I said — *I like William Burroughs & I really love Allen Ginsberg.*

Do you think you will write like Allen Ginsberg? he asked.

No, I said.

So you think you will write like yourself? he asked.

Yes, I said.

I waited for him to tell me that my writing would be rubbish & then I'd know he was an idiot. Because how can he possibly know that? I also thought if I said that I was going to write like these famous authors he would be likely to think I had *delusions of grandeur.* Don't you just love that phrase?

When the appointment came to an end he asked me if I was going to make another one.

I hesitated, thinking about it. He became exasperated —

You are meant to see if there is a rapport! he said.

I couldn't give a damn about a rapport. I was trying to figure out if he was an idiot or not.

I wanted to talk to someone sensible. He turned out to be a very helpful & sensible person.

Near the end of our sessions I gave him a story I had written about K that had been published.

You wrote a story & it has been published in a magazine? he asked, surprised. He was delighted & took it eagerly & read it.

You could see when he got to the end he tried not to cry. I loved him for that.

Fighting

We didn't really fight when we were very young. She made me angry in the science class one day, like I told you, when we were expected to cut up the dead rats that stank of formaldehyde. I remember being angry & it made my vision blurry. But we never really had any disagreements. It wasn't until we got to our thirties that things started to go awry.

I would come home from being out with her & have to lie on my bed & try & process the poison that she kept jabbing into me with her mean remarks. My house mate at the time saw me lying on my bed after coming back from being with her & she came in & said —

This is her shit! You can't let this get to you, it's her shit! I don't know how my house mate knew what was going on but she did.

It's hard to remember the details of what it was like — just endless sarcastic, bitter remarks. But it wasn't always like this. She got a job in a biddie home & she seemed very happy working there — at first. We were about thirty. She asked me if I was interested in coming to work there with her. I went to meet the manager & got a job & we worked together very well. That was when she was involved with The Grey Man as I've already told you.

A Snob from over the River

There was a time when I was living in South Yarra with some friends. I had agreed to meet her in a pub in Fitzroy — The Provincial — before it had been gentrified. She was with the guy that I told you about who said he'd been told three times she was dead. There was another woman there too who was very well off but tried to pretend she was a total bogan. She was addicted to alcohol. I know there are all kinds of versions of that but let's say that I only saw her sober once. And I saw her many times over the years. On the one time I did see her sober she was a very lovely person. I saw her in the street & had a chat with her & she was downright meek & childlike & gentle. Her family had bought her a house in Fitzroy but... well here's what happened.

I arrived & most of them were already half cut. We spoke & everyone seemed strained — but not Karen who was chipper & seemed glad to see me. Then one of the group (a man I didn't know) was so drunk he tipped his glass of beer over the table. He sat in a stupor & didn't realise it happened. The drunk woman started yelling at me —

Well? Go & get a cloth! Go & get a fucking cloth! Don't just sit there — looking pretty!

I didn't know it was my responsibility to clean up after the drunks. But she got up & went & got a cloth & mopped up the table. Dabbing at it in a rage. She sat down —

This is the real world & we are the real people, she said.

What brings you over this side of town says the 'three times she's dead' guy.

What is going on? I asked. They were obviously annoyed with me about something but I didn't know these people well & didn't know what I had done.

Karen told me later she had told them a friend of hers from 'over the river' was coming to visit. So they were well prepared to attack me for being a well-off snob. I had met them many times before but they didn't remember. They were better off than I was. But just turning up clean & neat & sober was enough for them to get their talons out.

When I was about nineteen I remember talking to Karen about class & I said —

I guess my family are lower middle — she took a puff of her cigarette & said — *not even that — working class migrants.* Class is peculiar in Australia. I have met many people who will never let you forget that you are not one of them. They are usually the children of professionals.

Now they are professionals too.

But some people will get annoyed if you say that your family are working-class migrants. *Dream on!* they say. Like it's a badge of honour you are claiming for yourself.

They do have pride about being working class in Britain. Here, a lot of comedy is about laughing at the plebs & what an ignorant bunch of fuck wits they are. When the comics are interviewed they make it clear that they think of themselves as posh & they put on their educated, slightly English, accents. But Australia sucks up to the Americans more than the English these days so the English accents have toned down a bit.

When I told my mum about how she set me up in the pub with her aggressive friends & she sat while they attacked me my mum wanted me to have nothing more to do with her. But mum, as I've told you, never liked her.

I did avoid her for a while but I stopped living in South Yarra & moved back to Collingwood so I guess, at that time, it was considered that I was back among the plebs.

Living in Fitzroy

Around the time that Karen was living in a flat above a shop in Fitzroy. It was hard on her children. She had Polly & Christopher. One day her little girl, Polly, who was a toddler, ran down the stairs & out onto Brunswick Street before Karen knew she had gone. When Karen saw she was missing she went running out & a woman had rescued Polly from off the road. When Karen went over to the woman to get Polly the woman went off at her — *The child was in the middle of the road & there was a tram coming one way & a tram coming the other way & cars everywhere! People like you should not be allowed to have children!* Karen never acknowledged to me that she felt bad about this she just said —

The woman was clearly really stressed out with what had happened.

It was as if she forgave the woman making such a remark — but she never let on that she felt responsible & guilty & terrified at the thought that anything could have happened to Polly.

Her son Christopher also told her that he wanted to stay most of his time with his dad & his dad's partner Helen. He was just a little kid & was upset by the chaos of the place.

He was really upset about deciding this & was worried about his mum. But she didn't let on to me about how awful this must have been for her.

Karen always said to me that I lacked self-confidence — which was different from self-esteem. I always thought & felt that the world would not value me in any way.

But she would give back as much as she got. It was rare for her to ever let on that someone had made her reflect on herself.

Even when she was pregnant with her children she did not respond to the medical staff who were for ever trying to get her to ease up on smoking. But, in some ways, I understood that she never wanted to give into 'them.'

Reading

I have found that when someone that you love dies it changes the way you read.

A philosopher I read once asks the reader to test if they are really committed to life.

Would we be prepared to live our lives over & over again, going over the same hurts & the same disappointments, perhaps the same physical pain. It is an intellectual exercise.

Before my father died my mum would say to him —

Would you stay with me for all eternity? And my dad would say —*Yes.*

For ever & ever? my mum would ask & my dad would say —*Yes, I would my dear, for ever & ever.*

But when I consider the great sorrow Karen experienced in life, could I agree to live my life over & over when I could only be bringing her with me? In saying 'yes' to your own life you are saying 'yes' to everyone's life.

Not everyone would say 'yes' to do it all again, over & over.

Many times she would be filled with a kind of wonder at the connections between us all.

She would say — *I wouldn't be dead for quids* to express wonder at the synchronicity of events that showed connections between people.

She often showed humanity to people & would encourage & support them. These same people were often angry with her later in their lives when they had recovered from their own hurts. I was one of them. She would support me through hard times but I was often, in later years, really angry with her.

I don't think the exercise of the imagination suggested by the philosopher takes into account the lives of other people connected to us. When I thought of myself, in my own selfish isolation, I would think about living life again & again. You would have to forget what you had done because it would be a hell of boredom right from the get-go. But my life would not be my life without other people. I don't know if Karen would want to come back.

I used to think that philosophy was interesting. Now I think there are only a few privileged voices that are allowed to be heard. They speak the same language & spend most of their time trying to tear down one another's systems. It's not about life & other people at all.

Mount Major

As I told you, when I was a child I grew up at Dookie Agricultural College. There was a mountain nearby & we would climb it.

The view from the mountain was a green, brown & yellow landscape with trees & farms & roads all around. I looked across as far as I could & what I couldn't see was Melbourne but I knew that was where my grandparents lived & I knew I was going there in the future.

The view from the mountain at that time was the future. Now, when I think of the view from the mountain, it is the past. I remember Karen & my grandparents.

Break

Karen & I had been fighting for a while & we had taken a long break from one another.

We fought on the phone. She rang up to confront me about why I seemed angry with her when I left her.

Why are you so angry? What have I done? I asked.

At first she tried to say that she didn't like going down Brunswick Street & I was always wanting to meet her there. She was implying that I was becoming a kind of yuppie wanker. I wasn't having it.

I don't know why you have all this subterranean venom, I said.

I am really angry with you about a lot of things, she said.

What are you angry about? I asked.

She got really annoyed & started yelling —*I don't see any point in opening up a whole can of worms.*

Well, I can't see you then, I said.

Fine! she said.

And we didn't see one another for a while.

I had moved out of the last group home & was living alone. It was during that extended time away from her, perhaps the longest we had ever been apart, that I began to understand that Karen had suffered something catastrophic as a child.

She had been suffering from when I first met her. I am not sure why this reality came to me then but I think it was connected with having a break from one another. When you have a break sometimes truths come to you.

It may also have been because there were a lot of changes in the culture around us & there was a lot of information about the abuse of children in the media at the time.

She would always present any of her behaviour as fixed & not to be challenged.

Once, when we were having a disagreement, not long after we had worked in the biddie home, she said to me —

But don't I know you better than anyone in the world & don't you know me better than anyone in the world?

I did not understand this remark & denied it. I thought she was being heavy & weird.

But when we had the break the knowledge that she had suffered something came to me as an understanding & while I don't know how it came into my mind I knew it to be true.

Maybe the quiet time put pieces together.

At the time there were a lot media stories about dodgy psychiatrists & psychologists 'implanting' false memories of childhood abuse.

When I saw Karen again I talked to her about her childhood. I don't remember how the conversation took shape. I didn't confront her with it. It was another of those strange synchronous times when she was thinking about it & I was thinking about it separately.

She talked to me about it & said that she was thrown by the media stories & they confused her. I asked her —

Do you mean you started to doubt yourself & whether it really happened?

She nodded & looked afraid & demoralised.

I can tell you that I think it is true, I said. She then told me that she had confronted him & 'he admitted it.'

It happened when her mum was in hospital getting tests. She was left without anyone to look out for her. She would have been 10 or 11. She was always a little proud that she had a 'precocious puberty' when she was about 10. It was like a kind of joke because everything else about her was years ahead of everyone too. But now I wonder why she had a precocious puberty.

I've have often thought there would be no way Karen would have taken him to court.

It would have been a most peculiar scenario for her to try to use *them* to help her. She avoided the powers as much as she could.

I've seen her angry with lovers. I've seen her angry with a Real Estate agent once who knocked her back for renting a house after meeting her. He had agreed to rent her the house — until he met her.

But I do not remember her holding onto any bitterness & resentment.

But there was a sadder reason she did not want to bring her abuser to the courts.

It went on for a short time. But that doesn't mean much. It could have been a thousand years. She described to me how she acted out the scene with The Grey Man. The Grey Man was reluctant but she told him what to say to her as he was doing it.

For most of this story I have told things as I saw & heard them but there are some things that have been told to me by other people & I think it is compelling enough to tell you here.

Karen's partner Jeremy told me that she wanted the rapist to admit to her what he did when she was a child &, more importantly, to acknowledge the impact it had on her. She wanted him to acknowledge this so that she could forgive him & there would be a scene of redemption & reconciliation. Because she claimed to love him.

There would have been no historical sexual abuse claim, Jeremy said — *because she loved him.* But when she confronted him & tried to get him to admit the pain & damage that it had done, all the confusion it created in a child, all he could say was — *You were only upset when I stopped.*

Jeremy tells me that she tried several times to get him to understand the effect it had had on her but no, he never would admit it. He would just hurt her again & again by acknowledging the event but not the trauma it created.

I remember when we were children asking her why she loved this man. I could not see any redeeming qualities in him. Miyazaki's characters have good & bad in them. It is one of the reasons I love his films so much. There is no black & white. Even though you may think it absurd to compare this dark situation with an anime film — it is in his art more than most that the complexity of character is expressed — more than in the usual dramas involving real people.

I wish I could be like Miyazaki & say that I saw something good & kind in him. I do remember that he was a giggler. He would laugh at things. But he took no interest in her or her life.

I would ask her — *why do you love him?* And she would always reply — *because he's all I've got.*

I never could get it — I wanted her to kick him to the kerb even before I knew what he had done. When we were very young I used to think it was him she was talking about when she talked about always being defeated by *them.* That fighting was just an annoyance to them because they would always win.

When I have discussed this with men she was close to they say —

O yeah, Karen told me about what happened immediately when I got involved with her or —

Karen had trauma she could not recover from.

They think of it as an event, they have a name for it. It is labelled & compartmentalised. That's not how I see it at all. It may not be the whole answer — the psychiatrist said to me that life is more complicated than in the movies. In the movies there is a puzzle about a character & then there's an answer. I am not saying that what happened to her as a child explains everything. But it was a lot of what was going on with her when I first met her. I cannot label it & put it away.

I also think she protected me from the dark. It could have been because she thought I was too daft to get it. It could have been that she did not trust me to believe her & take it seriously. But I usually believed her eventually — despite all her howling lies. It could have been that she was still very confused herself about what had gone on.

But the knowledge came to me as in a dream & I knew it to be true.

What is the love they are always talking about in this culture? Love that seems always sacrificing. Karen & I would talk about the difficulty women had leaving men who abuse them.

The feminists that we were mixing with at the time would often emphasise that life was very difficult economically when you left a partnership or marriage. They would talk about how socially difficult it is when you have children. Karen didn't think sufficient account was taken of the truth that women often love these men. Love is hard to get out of. Maybe it's harder to get out of if you grew up with no foundation in it.

There is a woman called Jane Elliot who does the Blue eyes/Brown eyes documentaries.

In one of the documentaries she says —

You can stick your love where the sun don't shine, I want change, behavioural change.

I think of this when people make the claim that they love but behave like they do not. But it takes a lot of effort to get away & it is much more difficult when they are a family member or when you have children.

When I go to weddings they talk about the kindness & patience of love & they read out the love described in Corinthians. They've made Corinthians into a cliché.

Just like at funerals they will play *You are the Wind Beneath My Wings.* My dad said he was sick to death of listening to this song at funerals.

Mum & dad both agreed with me when I said I don't think sexual love has anything to do with Corinthians kind of love.

But Corinthians says that love rejoices with the truth.

Children

Only twice in the whole time we were friends I managed to surprise & silence her, take charge of the story — she always took charge of the story. The two times were about children.

I love my nephews & have had a lot to do with them growing up. I have often told them they are the best things that have happened in our lives, that is, the lives of their parents & me.

Karen had four children: Christopher, Polly, Eurydice (Ridi) & John (Johnny). She would always say that the worst thing that can happen to a person is if something happens to their children.

Ridi was seven when Karen died. Johnny was only about 18 months old.

Ridi was, of course, very upset & angry for a long time after her mum died.

But the children had very good people in their lives who looked after them. Jeremy, Tim & Helen & Judy — Judy had co-parented Polly. Judy is one of those people who does quiet good things for people all the time & doesn't seem to realise what a profoundly good person she is.

When I met Karen in a café one day in Brunswick Street she was talking to me about whether methadone would affect the baby she was carrying — the baby that was to be Ridi.

Oh come on Karen, I said — *we both know you are doing more than methadone.*

She stared at me. I stared back. *You are really freaking me out*, she said and laughed a little. But she never denied that she was still using.

The other time that I stopped her was when we were sitting having coffee & talking & she said that thing to me I told you about — *It's now or never for you for children isn't it?*

She was shocked that I stood up to her trying to take me down.

When Ridi was a little girl Karen talked about how very beautiful she was with her long dark red hair. She thought for sure with her beauty &, perhaps because of things she saw in Ridi's nature, she would become an actor — that she liked to perform.

We're Running Out of Options

It must have been when she lost her job in the public service. We must have been in our late thirties. She said she wanted to work in the public service for ten years. But I think she lost that job because she was caught working & collecting the pension.

It was lucky she escaped jail.

The last plan she had was to be a teacher.

I think I'd make a great teacher, she said.

She would have. She would have been able to explain things clearly to children. She would have had a great understanding of what they needed. I didn't say anything when she said she wanted to be a teacher. I had lost hope that she would stick at anything. She had dropped out of schools & university & jobs.

But some of her stories about her work in the public service I loved. She was working in what was then called the Department of Social Security. There used to be a Commonwealth Employment Service, which helped people find jobs, but this was privatised & billions in public money went to the new Job Network Providers (JNP's). There have been a few investigations into some of these private agencies & some of them have had to pay back millions but the system remains.

If you apply for the dole you will be allocated to one of these 'providers' who will send you on useless courses & make you go to meetings — like 'job club' where you get to sit with other people who are artists & musicians & people who have mental health problems & discuss things like positive thinking. One woman who ran one of these classes spent most of her time talking with us about her personal grief over the death of a family member.

I have had some funny times in these meetings because some of the characters that get sent to them are hilarious. One musician, when asked by the person in charge what we should do when we are all despairing about being unemployed said — *Eye of the Tiger?*

Another one had on a t-shirt with a picture of Jimmy Hendrix & the words Bob Marley written underneath it. I had never seen this before, don't know who thought it up, but it was funny to see in one of those meetings & I kept giggling for ages.

Once I got sent to a psychologist who made me fill out personality test forms & assessed me as needing to retrain as an engineer. Not an engineer who gets bridges to stand up but one who goes around fixing televisions. This was before everyone got their TV through the net. When I went back to the Employment Service (before it was the JNP) the case manager bloke said to me — *we pay these people (psychologists) a lot of money — tell me — did you get anything out of it*?

I said no. She was another box ticker. One JNP I saw always said — *we don't make the rules.* She said this to me three times. I could hear her saying it to people on the phone. She would say it to her colleagues. Irritated, I made up my mind to tell her that's what fascists say & then I never got the chance because she didn't say it again.

But Karen worked in the section that administered claims for 'social security.' Social security is the money that is meant to keep you off the streets. Keep you socially secure. Socially secure by being given less than half of what is the estimated poverty line.

There was a young woman came into her office & Karen was at the front counter. The woman was trying to find work & was not having any success. She looked away from Karen & out the window & she was sad & very demoralised & said —*I don't know, I just don't know — whether there is a job out there for me.*

Karen said — *Yes, I know but sometimes you know a job isn't everything. You have to give up things to have a job. Some days you wake up & it's cold & it's raining & you think how much you would love to stay at home & stay in bed for a little longer.*

It would have been a very lovely thing for the young woman to have someone sympathise with her in such an environment.

Another time she was called to a meeting with her 'superiors' who asked her to account for the fact that, despite all the years she had been working in the Department, she had never 'breached' anyone — that is — knocked them off benefits because they had not complied with a meeting or whatever.

That is marvellous, that is just what I would have expected of you, I told her when she told me this story.

I cannot imagine her ever doing anything mean to people like that. She would never go along with a fucked-up system that tortures & penalises the most vulnerable & poor.

But she lost her job or stopped working there. That must have been terrible for her. Losing the money & security.

We are running out of options, she said to me one day. And she did mean the both of us. We were in our thirties. Another time she said — *You are probably unemployable by now.*

She always wanted to take me with her

Love again

It was her final project when she met & got involved with Jeremy. We had known Jeremy since we were at university. He is and was an exceptionally lovely character & very intelligent. He was always great to talk to about all sorts of topics but his particular interest is politics & so we would cross paths quite a bit with our involvements with the left.

When we were in our mid 30's she had been back in touch with him because he was involved with a legal/political case.

She came around to my flat & told me —

O my god — I've got a girly crush on Jeremy.

I groaned, not because it was Jeremy, but because I thought it was going to be another drama of hers.

Very soon they were in a love affair. That gave her something to do. They decided they were going to have a family — perhaps five children if they could — & she talked about having trip-el-ets & said the word in that way.

Sometimes when I speak with Polly about that time Polly tells me that she was exasperated with her mum having more children.

I think her plan was that she would have children & Jeremy would go out to work. But I think she found looking after the children more demanding than she realised. She told me once she didn't know how she was going to get through the day.

It was after Karen had Ridi that she went to find her biological father again. She had found him many years before &, unlike the reaction of her biological mother who, for whatever reason, did not want to keep in touch with her, her father had a family & they were delighted that she had tracked them down. They wanted to bring her into their family. She found that she had half-brothers & sisters & they were all very friendly & welcoming to her. But she said to me — *It was too much for me, I couldn't handle it, I felt like I didn't deserve it or something.*

When she found her biological mother her mother was living in the type of place where Karen would love to live. The house was old & had all sorts of animals in the garden — dogs & cats & chickens. Her mum had the same hair colour & the same laugh. She was excited about finding her mum.

She also thought it was peculiar that her mother was living in the same kind of house that Karen would have loved. It was beyond sad to me that she had to leave her mum as a baby & go & live in a completely different world — full of money & pain. After this meeting it was arranged that her mum would contact her & have Karen come around for dinner.

But when the time came for her mum to call — she never did. Karen shrugged & looked sad. I just couldn't believe it.

But this was not what happened with her dad.

It was not until after she had Ridi that she felt able to go back & see her father & show him her new little girl.

But he had died.

She rang me — we talked & I whinged about some problem or other — then she said —

He's dead! Dead! And she told me about her father.

Her sisters had tried to comfort her —

We tried to find you everywhere, they said. *You do know that he loved you Karen, he really loved you,* they said. But she thought it was one more dreadful trick life had played on her — when she was finally able to meet him & show him her new baby — he was gone. I am not sure if she had any contact with that family again. I only saw Karen a few times after she had Ridi. I was involved in helping to look after my nephews. There were only a few times after that I met her in cafés with the children.

One of our saddest meetings was when we were on our own & we were sitting outside a café in Brunswick Street. I got up to go to the toilet & she said to me —

Are you going to trust me with your handbag? I looked at her.

It was amazing she would think of herself as someone who would steal from me.

It was out of the realm of what I thought of her.

Yes, I am, I said.

The last phone call we had she rang up late one night & was really upset because her dad (the adoptive one) had had a heart attack & was in hospital.

My god you sound really out of it Karen, I said. She sounded very sedated & her voice was slow.

He's had a heart attack & he might die. My brother said — don't call Karen — she's not family! She told me.

That's just ridiculous! Of course you are family, I said.

I was thinking this would be very hard for her, *really* hard for her, that it would remind her of her mum.

I just really need to know that you & Patsy will be there for me if anything happens, she said.

If he dies & I have to go to the funeral, will you & Patsy be there for me?

Yes, of course we will be.

She said she had to go. I said — *You ring me any time, okay?*

Thank you darlin, she said.

And that was the last conversation I had with her. I asked Patsy if she had rung him & he said she hadn't. Maybe she was more sure of him. We had fought so often in the last few years & even after this phone call, after a few days, I went back to being angry with her again.

Jeremy told me recently that they were under a lot of stress (being together) & they were coming to the end. Or he was. She would have known that.

Eurydice

When Eurydice was born I thought it was a stupid pretentious name. Then I felt guilty for saying so to my friend Katie who is 1000 times kinder than me. Karen asked me if I thought it was too much & I never let on that I did. But the name quickly stuck. I didn't have much involvement with the children she had with Jeremy. We used to have picnics once a year & then I would see them. We took Johnny & Ridi out a few times after Karen died, to the zoo & places like that, but that petered out & we mostly just saw them about once a year.

I would sometimes go to plays that Ridi was in — she wanted to act & be involved with theatre from when she was very young.

The last time I saw her was about a month before she died.

She had been practicing for a long time with her stand-up comedy but she didn't want anyone, like family types, to go & see her. Then, finally, she did allow us to go & so I went down to the Highlander Hotel, in Highlander Lane, off Flinders Street to see her.

My friend Katie met me there later. While I was waiting I got a drink of wine & joked with the barman about 'Glasgow Kisses' & then I ordered a snack of haggis balls that came with a spicy sauce.

I was eating these & thinking how very unScottish was the spicy sauce but loved that someone in Melbourne was making these dishes & thinking how strange a co-incidence it was that Ridi would be working in a pub run by Scots.

When she arrived she looked really happy & said —

Elaine! You came! & I said — *Yes of course I did!*

It was lovely to see her & for her to allow us to watch her perform.

When Katie arrived we went upstairs & we sat in the front row. Ridi & I looked at one another throughout the performance. That's how it felt to me. I kept nodding & willing her to keep it together & keep being great at it.

I am always overawed by comedians — how they have the courage to stand up in front of people & speak. Sometimes I don't laugh at their jokes but still I am enchanted that they have the courage.

I thought her delivery was marvellous. I had heard she was planning to go to London to do performances there. She made jokes about her name & talked about how funny it was that her parents gave her a complicated name — when her brother's name was — John! She also talked about how hard it was for her to say her name when she had what the speech therapists called 'slushy s's' or a lisp.

That made me feel better about being mean about her name when she was born.

As she was standing there I was thinking how wonderful it was she had the nerve to stand up in front of people like that & how great she was. It was a new day & good things were going to come to the family. This was something I could talk to Ridi about & I wanted to tell her all about her mum.

When we got up to leave she was standing at the door with her donation bucket & I asked her if she minded if I gave her a hug & she said of course. I gave her a kiss & hug & told her how fabulous she was & how great her timing & delivery were.

A few weeks later her dad sent me a text to say that I may be worried about Ridi because there was a young woman killed in the Carlton gardens — & it *was* Ridi. When I got to that part of the text I did not read on but rang him immediately. Later I saw he had also said it was probably better if I did not ring just at that moment.

I would see the film on television of them carting a body off the park grounds covered in a sheet. My thoughts could not go to the reality of Ridi being under the sheet.

After a few days Polly rang me. The family were on their way to the morgue to identify the body. She was lovely & friendly & asked if I was alright & that Jeremy had asked her to ring because I had been upset on the phone. I couldn't comprehend how they could be so considerate of me when they must have been in an agony of grief.

Jeremy & Johnny had to move out of the house because the media were going berserk.

On the morning that she died two police came to Jeremy's door & it was early morning & they yelled at him —

Stand back, stand back, we have pepper spray.

Jeremy told me it took him a few moments to take in the reality & he thought it was some of Ridi's comedy friends having a joke. It took the police a while to realise that Jeremy was Ridi's father & not a guilty partner.

There was quite a commotion in the community & in the media. There was a candlelight vigil in the park with many people attending. I did not go. I saw the politicians there & many people were upset. I just don't understand. Why is being murdered in the park by a stranger more terrible than being murdered by your husband or partner? I asked people & they tried to explain to me that being murdered by your partner is more understandable. I don't think so.

If I had a family member die that way I would be just as shattered. I don't understand at all.

People did talk about women & violence against women generally & they banged on about how we ought to be able to walk the streets at dark. I've never been afraid of the dark.

The women who are murdered in their homes — aren't they murdered in the light?

Everyone likes to think they are in control of their own destiny. They like to think they are different from women who are killed by their partners & they would have left before it got to that. But doesn't it often get to that *because* they leave?

A lawyer I met once said about a client —

O she said — I think he really loves me anyway — like I've heard about 1000 times from women who are assaulted & they'll go back & it will continue.

A friend of mine said — *Yeah, & he hears it 1000 times because the men won't stop hitting them.*

And in the beginning they did indeed try to blame Ridi for walking through the park — what was a young woman doing walking through the park late at night? Then, when people found out it was because she was coming home from performing, they eased up a bit.

She had a legitimate reason for being there.

But some people said stuff to me like — she could not have had any real concern & respect for herself to walk alone though a park at night.

Some people got shitty that there was a fuss about her & thought it was because she came from North Carlton — but then they eased up when they realised it was from the commission flats in North Carlton & not from a yuppy privileged household.

He saw her from around Flinders Street & Elizabeth Street & picked her out & followed her & attacked her from behind & killed her.

When I went to the funeral I tried to stay back when the family walked in. Jeremy said — *Come & sit with us Yane, you are a part of our family,* which was a very kind thing to say.

I started to cry when I saw the front of the order of service because there was a beautiful picture of Ridi & a quote from the song *Rebel Girl* by Bikini Kill. I love that song & I didn't know she loved that song.

I had been to see the family a week before the funeral. Polly already had a sophisticated view about the media commotion. She told the family — that (the media event) is a very separate thing to us. The celebrant was there when I arrived.

Thank you so much for choosing me, she said. *I am so honoured. How did you find me?*

We all looked at her.

Christopher looked in the phone book under celebrants and saw you there, said Polly.

Christopher, Karen's first son, turned up a bit later & so he missed the celebrant asking what music the family were going to play when they lowered the coffin into the ground. Jeremy said he didn't want any music.

It's just that it is a bit morbid to have a coffin lowered into the ground without any music, the celebrant said.

Well, I think there's just no getting away from the fact that a coffin being lowered into the ground is morbid, said Jeremy.

We told this to Christopher when he arrived and we laughed.

But when we got to the grave & when the coffin was lowered into the ground it took ages.

It would have been good to have some music instead of the creaking of the gadget that lowers the coffin. Before they lowered the coffin Jeremy went over & touched it & bowed & nodded a little. It was a gesture of great tenderness & respect for his daughter. All those years that he had looked after her & spoken with her & survived Karen's death with her. And all the promise & individuality she had shown & now gone. People went over to throw a flower into the grave but I couldn't do it when everyone was there. I thought I would lose my balance.

When everyone had moved away I went over to put a flower in & I looked down into the grave.

It was a long way down.

I thought — *Ridi is in that box. Ridi will be here for ever now.*

Jeremy told me that when Karen died he felt her absence immediately. I did not feel it immediately but, of course, I was not living with her. It felt as if she was with me for a long time after her death.

I saw that lovely woman interviewed who played piano in the city — Natalie Trayling — you can see her interviewed on YouTube. She had a daughter called Karen who died in a car accident & another who died of cystic fibrosis. Listening to Ms Trayling speak is like listening to poetry. She says she does not feel that death is the end. She has never felt that her children have gone. They are always with her. I wish I could say the same about people I know who have died. Sometimes I feel that they are with me but, for most of the time, when I think of them, I don't feel that they are. Ridi's death makes you realise how unfair life can be. It was very difficult to take in the reality that she had gone because she was very young & there was a lot of unlived life.

When young people die there is a feeling that whatever they were here to do has not been finished & it is harder to face the truth that they are not waiting somewhere to come back & complete their life. My father was very close to his little brother who was eleven when he died in an accident. I wonder if my father had this feeling. He talked about his little brother towards the end of his own life.

The death of Karen's child was the only time I felt angry with Karen after she had died. *How could you have gone? How could you have gone & left your children? You should have been here to protect them.*

But then I remember how much she must have hated herself at the end. Many people she was close to were angry with her & I know there are countless stories of how she let them down & she must have known she was letting them down — & continued to do it.

I have learned that people can be very disappointing when someone has died. Sometimes they are so disappointing it is funny.

When my grandmother was dying, she was dying in my aunt's house, a friend of my grandmother's came to see her. When this friend was leaving the house she got to the front door she turned to my aunt & asked — *What newspapers will the death notices be in?*

We don't know that yet, said my aunt.

Many people were very disappointing when Ridi died. People tried to exploit her death which had attracted a lot of attention in the media

& other people were unable to take it in that I knew her & had been very close to her mum & she wasn't a public figure to me.

But you can't beat the TV.

Not everyone behaved like an idiot. One teacher at the uni — Jill — by chance I had to see her the morning after Ridi died. It had not been announced publicly who it was they had found in the park.

Jill was sitting at her computer & looking at the news & she said —

My god I am just looking at the news that a young woman has been killed in the park & I thought it might be my niece.

I told her it was someone I knew. She put her hands to her face & said —

O my god Elaine, the whole world has changed.

Because I had known Ridi's mother for many years — it made me feel like most of my life had been leading up to this catastrophic event. It felt like life is framed by the diabolical things people do.

But then I think that these are not the only things in life. Life is full of wonder.

Perhaps a peculiar, fantastical thing to say in such circumstances. Perhaps your brain immediately tries to balance things up.

But I have had luck & one piece of luck is that I had a charmed childhood.

When I was a child I used to walk in the countryside. I would walk alone with the dog. The dog always looked very pleased & happy to be bounding along through the grass.

He would sneeze at the grass seeds, because the grass was long, but he still loved it.

I had the sense of a benevolent presence. I don't know what it was. It could have been the dog. I never felt alone. My feelings of loneliness & isolation came in early youth when I spent too much time with people I had nothing in common with.

I will miss Karen always. I am certain her children will too.

I will miss sitting in a cinema watching a movie, like when we were watching the film *Pretty Woman,* & turning to her & saying —

O my god I feel really depressed — how do you feel? And she replied —*Yeah, suicidal.*

And then, when we left, we would laugh & laugh at what a dreadful film it was with values we did not share.

I will miss that we both loved expressions like 'mutton dressed as lamb' to describe women who present themselves as younger than they are & how people would put them down with this expression. We were going to be muttony lamby together when we got old.

I miss going to art exhibitions with her — like when we went to see Odilon Redon at the art gallery. I think we were looking at Bits of Rainbows —

Lets go see the flowers with the 'orrible 'eads she would say & laugh.

It's crazy that I miss her after all these years isn't it? And for sure it is pure selfishness.

I miss being able to run to her, when I was young, with every crisis & every problem & the profound understanding she would show me. I miss the old age that I might have had —we would have watched YouTube clips of interviews with Bertie & remembered how we loved him. She would have found the internet full of genius & beauty.

We would have wandered & talked & laughed & thought of ways to cause trouble.

I miss the love she had for me that I never understood & never felt the need to understand.

I miss standing in her front garden looking at her with a telegram in her hand. A telegram that told her she was loved by friends unknown. A telegram she thought she had to send to herself.

But, of all the images & memories I have of us, the one I love the most I didn't even know existed.

It was caught in a photograph taken by Patsy.

I don't have the photograph anymore & I hope Pat has the negative.

We are in her flat in Ivanhoe & we must be about 16. The whole photograph has a kind of strange glow. Maybe the open fire was behind us. We are sitting on the floor side by side. We look as if we've been laughing & Karen has her head resting on my shoulder, as if she put it there for a moment, & her long red hair is around her face. She is looking at the camera with a face full of joy. In that moment we are safe and happy & home.

Acknowledgments:

I would like to express my gratitude to the following people for their encouragement and support in writing this book —

Daniele Cerretti, Thérèsa Radic, Omega Pott, Yumiko Hirokawa, Karen Holl, Katrina Sawyer, Rachel Kennedy, Robert Sawyer, Joshua Sawyer, Norman Fell, Sandy Lie, Kim Fuentes, Alison Bessell, Anne McDermott, Jeremy Dixon, Polly Cotton, and my mum — Elizabeth Fell.

Karen Walters

www.ingramcontent.com/pod-product-compliance
Lightning Source LLC
Chambersburg PA
CBHW032008040426
42448CB00006B/536